Jung & Frodo

PRAISE FOR ROBIN ROBERTSON'S OTHER BOOKS

Beginner's Guide to Jungian Psychology

The world of consciousness has its spokesman in Robin Robertson. He's becoming a "name brand" when it comes to explaining in fresh terms the important mysteries that lie within us. Use his book as a guide and you'll discover within yourself the buried treasure that already knows your name!

- Psychologist and Writer Henry
Reed.

The Shadow's Gift

This is an unusually intelligent and accessible contribution to the 'self-improvement' literature. Robertson is a Jungian-oriented psychologist who demonstrates a profound and personal grasp of the intricacies and benefits of recognizing and engaging with shadow issues. He neither trivializes nor mystifies the power and dynamics inherent in such an engagement and his choice of material to amplify and illustrate his thesis – that the shadow is essential to our wholeness and need not be feared and excluded.

- Journal of Analytical Psychology.

At the End of Time: Prophecy and Revelation: A Spiritual Paradigm.

Robin Robertson continues to be one of the best writers about Jungian psychology in contemporary times, exploring complex ideas in clear, straightforward fashion. Yet he never dumbs the material down, respecting the intelligence & curiosity of the reader to follow where he guides. It's just that he has a deceptively conversational prose style that draws the reader in immediately & comfortably, while unfolding one rich & nuance concept after another, and showing how they all connect.

- William Timothy Lukeman, Amazon.com.

Jungian Archetypes: Jung, Gödel, and the History of Archetypes

Dr. Robertson is able to put high-order theory into simple, elegant, comprehensible prose. He is not only good at this; he is genuinely gifted.

- Dr. Michael Washburn, S.U.N.Y Press.

Mining the Soul: From the Inside Out

Dr. Robin Robertson is a masterful teacher who weaves the threads of brain research, Jungian psychology, mysticism, meditation and magic in a way that entertains and informs. I found myself utterly intrigued with his unique insight into that pair of opposites: inner and outer. This fine book is for the professional who wants a new and really good tool for his psychological tool kit, and for the lay person who wishes to learn how to penetrate the mysteries of the psyche. Robertson speaks with authority, clarity, humor, and depth.

- Gilda Frantz, Co-Editor, Psychological
Perspectives.

Indra's Net: Alchemy and Chaos Theory as Models for Transformation.

Robertson has a deft touch. His descriptions of both alchemy and chaos science are extremely clear. He manages to delineate each discipline clearly without compromising the dignity of either the ancient or modern science. . . . In shot, this is a beautiful and insightful book, and is itself a model of how to make use of science as an analogy to spirituality with integrity.

- Andrew Philip Smith, The
Gnostic-3.

Robertson states that central to the understanding of this book is the notion that, "the opus is within us as much as it is without". Robertson illustrates this through the complex but similar concepts held by ancient alchemists and contemporary chaos theorists. Robertson presents us with a world on the edge of revolution, a world in which we no longer understand ourselves as isolated agents acting out series of mechanistic processes, but instead a world in which we give witness to complexity, chaos, and connectedness.

- Keith Morrison, World Futures.

OTHER BOOKS BY ROBIN ROBERTSON

Jungian Archetypes: Jung, Gödel and the history of archetypes

At the End of Time (3rd ed)

Beginner's Guide to Jungian Psychology

The Shadow's Gift (3rd ed)

Mining the Soul: from the inside out

Indra's Net: alchemy and chaos theory as models for transformation

Inner Voices: and other essays on Jungian Psychology

Chaos Theory In Psychology and the Life Sciences (co-editor with Allan Combs)

Jung & Frodo

7 Paths of Individuation
In *Lord of the Rings*

Robin Robertson

Published in 2016
Manyhats Press
846 N. Monterey Street
Alhambra, CA 91801
rrobertson@pacbell.net

First published in 2013 as a Kindle e-book

Library of Congress Cataloging-in-Publication Data

Robertson, Robin, 1944-
Jung and Frodo: 7 Paths of Individuation in
Lord of the Rings / by Robin Robertson
Included bibliographical references and index

ISBN-13: 978-0692777503 (Manyhats Press)
ISBN-10: 0692777504

1. Jung, C. G.   2. Tolkien, J. R. R.   3. Lord of the Rings

Printed in the United States of America

Contents

Acknowledgments

I thank Taylor & Francis and *Psychological Perspectives* for permission to adapt a series of articles published in 2007, 2008, 2009, under the group heading "Seven Paths of the Hero in *Lord of the Rings.*

Grateful acknowledgment is made to Houghton Mifflin Harcourt for permission to quote material from *Lord of the Rings*, within the fair use limits of such quotes.

Acknowledgment is also made to Princeton University Press for permission to quote material in the *Collected Works of C. G. Jung*, again within fair use limits.

Introduction

J. R. R. Tolkien's *The Lord of the Rings* is the story of a quest, but it's a quest like none before it. It is a hero's journey in which not one hero, but several emerge. Each is faced with a set of challenges unique to his personality. Each takes a different path toward achieving his destiny, while simultaneously serving the greater goal of the quest: the fight against the great darkness that threatens Middle Earth.

Tolkien tapped archetypal roots to create these characters. Because we each contain those archetypes, we also contain all of Tolkien's characters within us. But no man/woman is all men/women. Though each of the heroes' stories speaks strongly to all of us, and each mirrors some part of development we must all ultimately pass through, we are likely to respond most strongly to a particular one of these heroes. We may laugh at Merry and Pippin, thrill to the wisdom of Gandalf, gasp at the revealed majesty of Strider/Aragorn, be touched by Gimli's adoration of the Lady Galadriel, watch in wonder as Legolas runs effortlessly across the top of snow-capped mountains, suffer with Frodo as the weight of the Ring grows ever heavier, and perhaps even weep at the loyalty of sweet Samwise. But one in particular will stand out for each of us as a favorite, an ideal. We can each find our heroic ideal pictured in *The Lord of the Rings*, yet we can also each contain all its heroes among the possibilities hidden within us. "In the long run," as P. L. Travers, the author of *Mary Poppins* says, "whatever it may be, every man must become the hero of his own story; his own fairy tale, if you like, a real fairy tale."[1]

Psychologist Carl Jung coined the term: *individuation*. Individuation is the process of becoming an autonomous individual separate from the collective values around us. Individuation is the process of becoming the person we are intended to be, our true self. An alternative term for this process which Jung also used and which has become widely adopted in recent years is *self-realization*. Psychologist Abraham Mallow coined still another term for this process: *self-actualization*.

However, it is important to realize that the "self" to be "realized" and/or "actualized" is something more than the ego; it is a transpersonal Self of which the ego is only a part. "Becoming the person we are intended to be" assumes that we each are born to serve a higher purpose; Jung called it our "myth" and said that we each have to discover our myth. When we individuate, we do more than bring together all the scattered aspects of our individuality into a comfortable whole. Individuation requires looking deeply into the darkness inside each of us, a darkness that goes beyond our existence as individuals. We have to descend into that darkness, fight battles within, then emerge once more into the light. And that is a lonely journey that few undertake willingly. But, as Jung says, a person has to "be alone if he is to find out what it is that supports him when he can no longer support himself. Only this experience can give him an indestructible foundation"[2]

Because individuation by its very nature drives a person to find himself or herself as an individual, it often brings the person into conflict with the collective values of society. Critics have often confused this process with an egoistic desire for self-gratification. Responding to such criticism, Jungian analyst Marie-Louise von Franz responded that "such an attitude has nothing at all to do with narcissism or with egoistic individualism,"[3] because it transcends such values.

Maslow argued that we all have a hierarchy of needs. At the lower end are "deficiency" needs, where we require something that we lack: food, water, shelter, safety, love, recognition, etc. Once these needs are met, beyond them lie "growth" needs, culminating in the need for self-actualization. The desire for self-gratification, no matter what form it takes, comes from a deficiency, something we lack. Individuation necessarily forces us to find values that are beyond egoistic desires as much as they are beyond collective restrictions. Tolkien understood this distinction between egoism and individuation quite well; he regarded the values he presented through his characters in *The Lord of the Rings* as eternal values, values expressed by human beings (and Elves, Dwarves, Wizards and Hobbits) in their finest moments.

Stories about heroes and their quests fascinate us, because, whether we know it or not, each of us is a hero on a quest to fulfil our unique destiny; that is what Jung meant by individuation. Mythologist Joseph Campbell said that a hero might wear any of a thousand faces. In my own study of *The Lord of the Rings*, I saw that Aragorn's story was the classic story of the hero's quest. But Frodo is a very different type of hero. And, in fact, as I looked more closely, I came to identify seven different types of hero; each such path is represented by a major character (or pair of characters) in J. R. R. Tolkien's *The Lord of the Rings*.

Though it sounds like I arrived at this insight through careful analysis, in actuality it came to me in a dream. I woke one morning with a fully formed concept for the book you are reading. I knew that there were exactly seven paths and even knew the names for each path. Like Coleridge waking with the poem "Kubla Khan" already written in his mind, I wrote it all down as quickly as I could before it vanished.

As a Jungian-oriented psychologist, I have a deep and abiding respect for the inner world of dreams and fantasies. I honor my dreams and have recorded and mulled over many thousands of them over the years. But to have this gift from the unconscious was something special. *The Lord of the Rings* has been the most important book in a life filled with books. At many key moments I've let my life be guided by the courage and wisdom of its characters. I knew this deep insight given me was important and needed to be shared. I'm pleased to offer it to you with the goal that each one of us may attain our own full heroic stature. This isn't something I've created, or even something Tolkien has created, but instead something that comes from the deepest well-springs of the human spirit that speaks through us.

And so, too, it speaks through YOU. What is the character of the hero in YOU? Based on J. R. R. Tolkien's *The Lord of the Rings*, this book will help you connect with your own inner hero. Explore the seven different faces of the hero and seven paths that a hero might take to recognize the seven choices that each of us might make for our own lives.

The Path of Curiosity

Although at the start, the young Hobbits Merry and Pippin care only about creature comforts, they are also, like many young creatures, insatiably curious about anything and everything. It is that curiosity that drives their individuation process. In the early parts of the quest, they constantly cause trouble through their monkey-like curiosity, but that curiosity also leads them to encounter more of Middle Earth than almost anyone else in the book. As they accumulate experience, they grow morally as well. Ultimately these two small figures grow so strong that when they return to the Shire, and find it taken over by human thugs, they are able to easily set things right with no need for the help of any of their apparently stronger friends. The other Hobbits in the Shire have little interest in this quest business, but they recognize quality when they see it. To them, Merry and Pippin have become far more important figures than Frodo. Ultimately, in the days after the period of *The Lord of the Rings*, Merry and Pippin become almost legendary figures in the history of Hobbiton.

The Path of Opposites

Gimli the Dwarf and Legolas the Elf are opposites, like Earth and Air, Fire and Water. They are representatives of opposing races and cultures who have for millennia been, if not enemies, deeply suspicious of each other. No one is as rooted in the earth as a Dwarf, digging his tunnels, accumulating his wealth. No one is as airy as an Elf, bound not even by mortality. Yet over the course of the quest, Legolas and Gimli grow first to respect, then to love their opposite, until they are as inseparable as Merry and Pippin. Their path of individuation offers all of us the possibility of reconciling what seem like irreconcilable opposites within us.

The Path of the Wizard

A Wizard, one of the wise, must resist arrogance and serve those less wise. He must ultimately accept death willingly in order to save others, and in the process be transformed into the wisest of the wise. Saruman fails his test, while Gandalf passes. Gandalf the Grey becomes Gandalf the White, taking on Saruman's mantle. Where once Saruman was the stronger, now Gandalf easily surpasses his powers. But, at the end of *The Lord of the Rings*, Gandalf's time, the time of the Wizard, has passed, as has that of Gimli the Dwarf and Legolas the Elf; Gandalf crosses over the sea to the Undying Lands, where the Elves dwell in immortality. It is now the time for Men . . . and perhaps Hobbits. But we can each learn much from the Wizard's path.

The Path of the King

A king must be willing to first lower himself and live the life of a common man, before rising to his full stature. Boromir fails this test (he who should have realized that he was a Steward, not a king), but finally redeems himself in death. Strider/Aragorn fully passes his test and, unlike Boromir, does not die but instead triumphs over death, actually raising the Army of the Dead to help him in a great battle. After the Quest is completed and the Ring destroyed, Strider fully becomes Aragorn, reunites Gondor and Arnor, and is crowned King Elessar. His is the traditional path of the hero, one that can teach all of us many lessons about our own individuation. This would have been the ending of many another hero's journey, but not *The Lord of the Rings*, which is far wiser. There remains three final paths: of Gollum, Samwise, and Frodo.

The Path of Tragic Failure

Driven by greed and avarice, Gollum loses his identity, and is reduced to little more than desire for his "precious" Ring. Yet, even in failure, even while committing evil, Gollum plays an indispensable part in the Quest. Subdued, almost won over by Frodo's kindness, he leads Frodo and Sam to Mount Doom. There, in Frodo's final moment of weakness, it is necessary for Gollum to bite off Frodo's finger in order for Frodo's destiny to be fulfilled. Gollum's path might be seen as the modern equivalent of the Greek tragic hero: though fated to fail personally, he yet serves greater needs. We each have a Gollum within us—who among us has never experienced greed and avarice? We each have to treat the Gollum inside with the same kindness displayed by Frodo and the same firmness displayed by Sam.

The Path of Love

Sam's is the simplest yet most touching of all paths: his childlike loyalty and love for Frodo makes him the one person who never wavers in his task throughout the book. Though all the characters are engaged in momentous events, Sam always remembers that the sun coming up in the morning is a glorious sight, and that Hobbits have to eat. When Frodo can no longer even walk, and will not let Sam carry the Ring, Sam carries Frodo. Then, when Gollum joins them, Frodo's kindness has to be balanced by Sam's stern limits. Ultimately Sam's outcome is the happiest of all those on the Quest: he has been able to see the Elves who so fascinated him, able to serve as Frodo's companion on the greatest of all quests, and, at the end, able to return to his blessed Shire, to marry his loving Rosie, have many children and live happily ever after.

The Path of Transcendence

Then there is Frodo, whose path transcends that of any other hero in literature. Seemingly the least heroic, always aware of his own fears, and his own limitations, he nevertheless accomplishes more than any of the supposedly greater figures known as Elves and Dwarves, Kings and Wizards. When the great quest is complete, and everyone is satisfied at the outcome, Frodo alone knows no peace, for he can never again be whole. *The Lord of the Rings* is wise enough to recognize that there can be no happy ending for him. Frodo, like Hamlet, can find no peace on earth. He has been too damaged in the process, and has passed beyond all the normal hopes and desires of our world. At the end he is left to journey away with the Elves to a world that will undoubtedly fit him no better than this one. Beyond that, we presume he must find some new answer unique to Frodo, some way to transcend the limitations of life, as must each of us.

Over the course of this book, we will follow each of these paths. In ordinary times, few of us are forced to take paths as difficult as those of the heroes of *The Lord of the Rings*. But in these strange transitional days when the old world is passing away and the new has not yet appeared, perhaps we all have to take one or another of these paths as we journey toward the dark lands of Mordor and confront the darkness we find there. As we follow the seven paths taken in *The Lord of the Rings*, it would be well to remember that "there's more wisdom in a story than in volumes of philosophy."[4]

Chapter One
The Path of Curiosity

From the moment a baby is born, it is torn between its need for security and its curiosity about the world around it. Anything and everything is likely to capture a baby's interest, if only for a little while. But it can only turn its attention outward to the world when it feels safe. Because of this need for a safe place to retreat, a baby quickly learns to differentiate its mother's face and voice from everything and everyone else in that strange chaotic world. This is so important that in many species, this recognition of mother is carried at the genetic level. Nobel prize winner Konrad Lorenz spent a lifetime studying such "imprinting" behaviors in animals. For example, he found that "greylag goslings unquestioningly accept the first living being whom they meet as their mother."[5] In contrast, with a mallard, the first creature "that emits the right quack note will be considered as mother."[6] From that moment on, a baby of any species turns to its mother for nurture, safety, support, security. It is only from that place of security that a baby is able to take tentative exploratory steps out into the world. But oh how wonderful that world can be! Watch the delight in a baby's eyes when it plays with a new toy, the sense of triumph in a toddler as it begins to take its first steps. Its new knowledge and accomplishment provides a sense of power and achievement that, if life goes well, eventually develops further into wisdom.

But curiosity far too often dies and we lose our "sense of wonder" about the world around us. Perhaps that is as it should be, simply a mark of maturity. Mathematician and philosopher Rene Descartes wrote that "what we commonly call being astonished is an excess of wonder which can never be otherwise than bad."[7] In disagreement modern essayist Adalgisa Lugli views wonder "as a form of learning—an intermediate, highly particular state akin to a sort of suspension of the mind between ignorance and enlightenment that marks the end of unknowing and the beginning of knowing."[8]

Let me interject a personal note in support of the need for a sense of wonder about the world around us. I've been an amateur magician for most of my life. I've found that most people love to see magic; they turn off their adult preconceptions and once more experience the delights of childhood. But there is also a minority who look at magic tricks as puzzles that they have to solve, who get angry when they can't solve them. They come up with the most ridiculous solutions, solutions a magician would never use, but insist they are right because they can't abide not knowing how something works. Far too many people in our time look at the world that way. Even if we view the world as a puzzle to be solved, however, it is more like a series of Chinese boxes where, once we open one box, another is revealed inside. But this still doesn't do justice to the world around us; the world isn't inanimate, it is alive and we are part of that life. When we approach the world with a sense of wonder, it becomes numinous and we are enriched by our participation in it. When we try to reduce it to something we can fully understand, we ourselves are reduced in the process.

Some people are lucky enough to retain that sense of awe and wonder long after childhood has come and gone. Famed mathematician John Horton Conway, who is probably best known for creating the cellular automata game of Life, expresses that attitude toward life this way. "I like things that shine and that involves quite often that they're a bit trashy. The magpie just picks up a piece of plastic that's covered in gold. I have taste, but I don't exercise it very frequently. So I'm just as likely to be doing something that isn't really worth doing as something that is."[9]

The Hobbits Meriadoc Brandybuck (Merry), and Peregrin Took (Pippin) are just such wonderful creatures. Throughout *The Lord of the Rings*, we delight in their unceasing enthusiasm and humor, and most of all: curiosity. They offer a path that we can all follow to our advantage, a corrective to the hardening of the imagination that too often happens as we grow older, a path that leads to accomplishment and eventually to wisdom. But before we describe Merry and Pippin's path, we need to talk a bit about Hobbits.

ABOUT HOBBITS

Fully four of the nine members of the "fellowship of the Ring" are Hobbits: Frodo Baggins, Samwise Gamgee (Sam), Merry, and Pippin. And, though he was now too old to be a member of the fellowship, we shouldn't forget Bilbo Baggins, who started the whole affair when he stole the One Ring from Gollum more than a quarter of a century before Frodo was born.

Tolkien tells us quite a bit about Hobbits in the prologue and in appendix F to *The Lord of the Rings*. They're about half a man's height - a little under 3' on the average - which explains why the men in the book call them *Halflings*. The word "Hobbit" evolved from *holbytla* (hole-builder),[10] which undoubtedly comes from their affinity for living in holes in the ground, though, by Bilbo's time, "it was, as a rule, only the richest and the poorest Hobbits that maintained the old custom."[11] They are largely rural folk who share Tolkien's love of nature and dislike of machinery. They have little interest in books and book-learning, except for genealogies of Hobbits, which they find endlessly fascinating and can debate about for hours on end. And, as might be expected of such earthbound people, most are distrustful of anything to do with water: few could swim and only a rare Hobbit could board a boat without grave misgivings.

Hobbits are a happy, peace-loving people, fond of laughter and jokes (often rude); food, drink (six times a day if they can get it), and pipe-tobacco; parties and presents, which, as Tolkien says, "they gave away freely and eagerly accepted."[12] Since their custom is to give away presents on their birthday, rather than receive them, few days passed without some sort of present being exchanged. But Tolkien reminds us that, though peaceful, that didn't mean that they are not tough as nails when life demanded it, a quality we will see many times throughout the Quest.

Of the five Hobbits that concern us - Bilbo, Frodo, Sam, Merry, and Pippin - only Sam is wholly typical of Hobbits, sharing almost all their likes and dislikes, except for his deep desire to see Elves! The other four, though fond of their creature comforts, are also fascinated by the world outside the Shire (the lovely rural village where they live). But Merry and

Pippin are driven by youthful curiosity about anything and everything outside that comfortable world to a degree far beyond Bilbo and Frodo, much less Sam. They are, like John Horton Conway, magpies eager to pick up every shiny stone that they see along the way. Though eight years apart in age, Merry and Pippin are inseparable friends, and their path in *The Lord of the Rings* is a single path: the path of youthful curiosity.

THE JOURNEY BEGINS

Unlike the wonderful scene in the movie, "*The Lord of the Rings*: The Fellowship of the Ring", where Merry and Pippin steal fireworks from Gandalf at Bilbo's "eleventy-first" birthday party,[13] in the book we don't meet the pair until Frodo is ready to leave the shire, to begin his journey as the Ring-bearer. We are told that Merry and Pippin are not only each other's best friends, but Frodo's as well. At that point, Frodo is 50, Merry 36, Sam 35, and Pippin 28.

> *We need to remember, however, that Hobbits don't come of age until thirty-three, and live perhaps 50% longer than we and the run-of-the-mill men in the book do. The main men we encounter in the book, especially Aragorn, are exceptions to this rule. They are descended from the Elf-Friends, the Kings of Men (Dúnedain to the Elves), whose life span was three times that of a normal man. While the blood line is muted in all except Aragorn, they still live much longer than normal men. Elves are immortal. Dwarves live about 250 years on the average, though Durin I, the founder of Gimli's line, lived for well over a thousand years. And Ents , who we will discuss later in this chapter, are the most ancient race of beings still living in Middle Earth, though not immortal, as are the Elves. Thus we can consider Frodo to be a mature Hobbit, comparable to a man in his early 30's; Merry and Sam are like young men in their early 20's; while Pippin, is still a teenager in Hobbit terms.*

When a young male of any species has been nurtured properly and led to feel secure, they often manifest a self-assurance that borders on cockiness. We tolerate and even smile at that over-confidence because it is a wonderful thing to see the joy of youth, and also because we know that it doesn't last nearly long enough in most of us. As the journey begins, Merry and Pippin are presented as just such joyful, self-confident young Hobbits, full of pranks and mischief, ready for any challenge that life has to present.

Frodo has done his best to keep his burden to himself, pretending that he is merely moving back to his childhood home of Buckland, on the Eastern borders of the Shire. In actuality, Frodo intends Buckland to be merely a stopping-off point on the way to the Elvish land of Rivendell. Merry (and another friend, Fatty Bolger), have gone ahead with carts of luggage, and now Frodo, Sam and Pippin start off on foot, carrying their provisions with them. When Frodo only half-teasingly accuses Sam of giving him the heaviest bags to carry, ever loyal Sam is immediately ready to carry more himself. But Pippin will have none of that, telling Sam it's good for Frodo, who needs to lose some weight anyway. We immediately know that, while Pippin might be the youngest, he's a handful for anyone to deal with. We will see this quality over and over as the story progresses, both for good and for ill.

We also know from this exchange that Frodo and Pippin (as well as Merry) come from a different "class" than Sam, which we will see more clearly when we discuss Sam's Path.

By the time the three meet up with Merry at Frodo's new house, they have already had their first encounters with the "Black Riders," and talked with a group of wandering Elves. But this is all preparation for the journey to come. After a good meal at his new house (for Tolkien goes out of his way to stress just how much Hobbits like their meals), Frodo stumbles over his words as he tries to find a way to tell Merry and Pippin that he is not staying in Buckland, but actually leaving the Shire on a dangerous mission. The pair laugh at Frodo's discomfort and tell him that they have known all along what was happening. We begin to see how shrewd they are when Pippin tells Frodo that they'd noticed all year how he'd been "saying farewell to all your haunts."[14] So young doesn't necessarily have to mean naive.

When they assure Frodo that they have no intention of allowing him to leave without them, Frodo is deeply moved but tries to warn them that this is a very different business from Bilbo's "treasure-hunt." But they are already one step ahead of Frodo here, too. They not only know that he is leaving, but that he's leaving because of the Ring. Merry had once seen Bilbo put on the Ring and vanish in order to avoid meeting the dreaded Sackville-Bagginses along the road. After that, Merry kept his eyes and ears open and even once managed to briefly read some of Bilbo's secret journal which told of his adventures and of the Ring. He shared all this with Pippin. When, years later, they saw Frodo ready to leave on a secret journey, they guessed that it had something to do with the Ring and enlisted Sam's help in spying on Frodo. All in the interests of protecting Frodo from himself, you understand.

When Frodo wonders in dismay whether he can trust anyone, we see still another side of Merry and Pippin, as Merry tells Frodo that of course they can be trusted to stick by him, and to keep his secrets. But they can't be trusted to let him go on a dangerous journey alone, because they are his friends. And so they are, as we find out many times throughout the course of their journey. But as for their keeping secrets, well, that is another story entirely.

The bravado of youth has its dangerous side as well. At the *Inn of the Prancing Pony*, Pippin becomes too fond of the sound of his own voice and begins telling the story of Bilbo's fabulous birthday party, leading up to his mysterious vanishing act. Frodo knows that will perk up any whose ears are alert for a word of the One Ring. Frodo has to jump in, which leads to his own nearly disastrous vanishing act. All because Pippin hadn't yet learned when a secret needs to be kept, despite Merry's assurance to Frodo to the contrary.

Throughout the Quest, there is a continued back-and-forth between the joy that Merry and Pippin bring and the difficulties their curiosity and impetuosity creates. Once they have passed their first series of difficulties and arrived at Rivendell, even Frodo's near death at the hands of the Ring Wraiths isn't enough to stifle Pippin. While Gandalf and Elrond are grave, worrying about what must be done next, Pippin is his usual irrepressible self. When Gandalf admonishes him for calling Frodo "Lord of the Ring," with a reminder that "we are sitting in a fortress. Outside it is getting dark," Pippin blithely tells Frodo not to pay any attention to Gandalf. It's much too pleasant in Rivendell for gloom and doom. Rivendell is a place for songs and dances, not hand-wringing.

And perhaps it is just that joy in life that is needed by all of us. What better answer to the darkness that we all encounter along our paths?

THE FELLOWSHIP OF THE RING FORMS THEN DISSOLVES

When, at the Council of Elrond in Rivendell, Merry and Pippin insist that they be included in the Fellowship of the Ring, Gandalf unexpectedly supports them against Elrond, who wants them left behind (especially Pippin as the youngest). As so many times in the book, Gandalf has a prescient sense that the young Hobbits will have important roles to play in the Quest. Once on the journey, however, Merry's and Pippin's eagerness diminishes as they begin to fully realize that they are no longer in the security of the Shire. When they hear the wargs (wolves) howl, Pippin fears that he is a coward and confesses to Sam: "I wish I had taken Elrond's advice. I am no good after all."[15] Note though that he is willing to share his self-doubts with Sam; no actual coward could ever do so.

While curiosity drives youth out into the world, often the challenges they meet temper their initial enthusiasm, and their self-confidence alternates with fear and self-doubt. Some never recover from the discovery that they are not invincible. Emotional growth occurs when we are challenged by adversity and still manage to triumph over that adversity. And sometimes, the greatest emotional growth occurs when adversity triumphs over us, yet we learn that we can still survive, and that perhaps it is possible to lose a battle without losing the war.

Nothing can stifle Pippin's insatiable curiosity about the world for long. A little later, in the depths of the caves of Moria, he drops a stone down a well simply to see how deep it is, perhaps alerting the Orcs to the presence of the Fellowship (or perhaps, as we will see later, it was Gollum who alerted the Orcs). This is too much for Gandalf who rebukes Pippin: "Fool of a Took! This is a serious journey, not a Hobbit walking party. Throw yourself in next time, and then you will be no further nuisance. Now be quiet!"[16]

As the journey progresses, both Merry and Pippin frequently complain about their lot and wish that they had stayed behind. In Lothlórien, the Elven forest home of Galadriel, like any good earthbound Hobbit, Pippin complains about sleeping in trees and Merry confesses to an Elf that "I have never been out of my own land before. And if I had known what the world outside was like, I don't think that I should have had the heart to leave it."[17]

> *In youth, the life we know seems tame and dull, while the world beyond seems exciting. Curiosity about the world beyond starts us on our journey, and we imagine that we want to experience all of it. Yet the actual experience often proves harder than we had imagined, and the mundane world we left becomes colored in our minds until it seems like paradise.*

Their greatest accomplishment in the early stages of the Quest comes merely from their presence, not their action. After Boromir tries to steal the Ring from Frodo, thus forcing the dissolution of the Fellowship, he is deeply ashamed; when he is confronted by a suspicious Aragorn, however, Boromir is not yet willing to admit what he has done. But when the Orcs attack Merry and Pippin, Boromir's greed and duplicity vanish, and his great warrior spirit awakens. He sacrifices his life in his defense of Merry and Pippin, who are nevertheless taken by the Orcs. When Aragorn kneels by the dying Boromir, Boromir is now able to confess his sin. He dies in peace when Aragorn assures him that his home of "Minis Tirith shall not fall!"[18] Much later in the book, when Gandalf hears of Boromir's death, he says it wasn't in vain the young Hobbits came, since they managed to make Boromir redeem himself. And he adds that they will have other roles to play, by their actions as well as their presence.

CAPTURED BY THE ORCS

After being captured by the Orcs, Pippin once again wishes that he had never come, feeling that he's been useless, simply an object to be dragged along like a suitcase. He would wish to be saved, except that would take Strider and the others away from more important tasks. Mostly he just wishes he could find a way to get free.

Though this might seem like still more complaining, something important has changed inside Pippin. Now rather than simply complaining about his situation, he has turned his complaint upon himself, realizing that he has been a nuisance to the others, little more than a piece of luggage. When he wishes that Strider could free them, he stops that line of thought, as it would take Strider away from more important things. Instead he begins to wish that he, Pippin, could find a way to help himself. And he does.

Soon after, he finds a way to cut his bonds, yet is clever enough to keep this hidden from the Orcs. Then when an opportunity presents itself, rather than make a half-hearted attempt at escape, Pippin gets away just far enough to leave a treasured brooch, given him by the Elves, on the ground, where it might be discovered by Strider, Gimli, and Legolas. And, in fact, it is, though by then Merry and Pippin have escaped on their own.

Merry is worse off than Pippin at this stage, as he has been knocked unconscious and carried by the Orcs, truly like the piece of luggage Pippin imagines himself to be. When Merry finally regains consciousness, we see just how tough these little Hobbits are. His first words upon awakening are "Hullo, Pippin!. So you've come on this little expedition, too? Where do we get bed and breakfast?"[19] It takes a great deal of courage to make jokes at a time when our life is in danger.

Merry and Pippin together present a more formidable front than either does alone. They tempt a single Orc guard into thinking they know more about the Ring than they do, which leads him to spirit them away from the main body of Orcs. There fortune favors the well-prepared: when the Orcs are attacked by the Riders from Rohan and their Orc captor is killed, Merry and Pippin are able to sneak away during the battle. Though still far from friends or safety, lost in the middle of a land totally unknown to them, they tease each other as if out for a picnic. With no idea where else to go, they resolve to go into the Fangorn forest, which has a fearful reputation among many, including Hobbits.

We see over and over again, that while a little discomfort makes Merry and Pippin complain and wish they were back home, real adversity brings out the best in the pair, as it often does in all of us.

TREEBEARD AND THE ENTS

In the Fangorn forest, Merry and Pippin encounter a very strange creature: "a large Man-like, almost Troll-like, figure of at least fourteen foot high,"[20] with skin so much like the bark of a tree that he appeared to be a talking, moving tree. He explains that he is an Ent—called Fangorn (the name of the Forest) by some, Treebeard by others.

The Ents are perhaps the most original of all Tolkien's creations. They are the most ancient race in Middle Earth (though the individual Tom Bombadil is even older), perhaps older even than the Elves, who at one point in the book address Treebeard as "Eldest."[21] Once indistinguishable from trees, when the Elves began talking to trees to learn of their lives, the Ents awoke to discover that they were not trees, but shepherds of trees, capable of movement and language.

Throughout the myths and legends of virtually all cultures is an archetype of the Wise Old Man (and his feminine counterpart, the Wise Old Woman): a man who, by virtue of his long life, has come to possess knowledge that transcends his life as an individual and embodies the wisdom of the race. Such wisdom is found not merely through an accumulation of experience, but also through introspection, by looking deep within. In the words of eighteenth-century poet William Cowper:

Knowledge and wisdom, far from being one,

Have ofttimes no connection. Knowledge dwells

In heads replete with thoughts of other men;

Wisdom in minds attentive to their own.

- William Cowper, "The Task"[22]

Treebeard is not only the oldest and wisest of the Ents , he is perhaps the greatest embodiment of the wisdom of age in *The Lord of the Rings*, even more so than Elrond the Elf and Gandalf the Wizard, both of whom Treebeard knows and respects. As such he is the perfect complement to the youthful Hobbits, who sense his essential goodness and trust him immediately. When they first look into his eyes, they "felt as if there was an enormous well behind them, filled up with ages of memory and long, slow, steady thinking; but their surface was sparkling with the present."[23] Treebeard is as interested in Merry and Pippin as they are in him. The Ents have a long list (long even for Ents) which describes all the races, but nowhere on that list are Hobbits. He is utterly delighted at finding something totally new in the world and asks them question upon question about Hobbits and their life in the Shire. We see that, even after the nearly innumerable years of his life, Treebeard still retains *his* curiosity about the world around him.

In an exchange that perfectly captures the dichotomy between the wise old Ent and the impetuous young Hobbits, he is astounded when, without any reservation, Merry and Pippin tell him their full names, and remarks that "You *are* hasty folk."[24] He explains that for Ents , their name describes everything they are and all that has happened to them, and he has no intention of saying all that to them right now.

When we're young, we take our own existence for granted and don't yet think about who we are and how we fit into the greater scheme of things. Treebeard is teaching Merry and Pippin something the young have to learn: that they are an evolving product of the life they live. When Abraham Lincoln remarked that he didn't like a man's face, a cabinet member said that the man couldn't do anything about his face. Lincoln would have none of that and rejoined that "after a certain age, every man is responsible for his face." In other words, we are each responsible for our lives. The moral choices we make throughout the course of our lives are reflected in us so deeply that others can see them in our face, our voice, our walk, our every action. And, in the case of Treebeard and the Ents (as with many Native Americans and other people of the earth), in their name.

Though Merry and Pippin don't reflect on Treebeard's comment when he makes it, as the Quest progresses, we watch them grow through the moral choices they are forced to make. And, on a lighter note, we watch them grow physically because of repeated drinks of the Ent draught that is the staple of the Ent diet. "The effect of the draught began at the toes, and rose steadily through every limb, bringing refreshment and vigour as it coursed upwards, right to the tips of the hair. Indeed the Hobbits felt that the hair on their heads was actually standing up, waving and curling and growing."[25] Whether that draught might also give them some of the Ent capacity for introspection to complement their extraversion goes unsaid.

If Treebeard has a lasting effect on Merry and Pippin, their impact on him is even more pronounced. Roused by their youthful sense of right and wrong, he realizes that he has slumbered far too long. He has allowed the wizard Saruman's evil to grow to the point where Saruman is now destroying the trees that the Ents protect and herd. After a war council that for Ents is remarkably "hasty," the Ents march on Saruman's stronghold of Isengard, which they rip to shreds, leaving Saruman isolated in his tower, surrounded by a moat the Ents dig and flood.

We will, regretfully, not describe the great battle of the Ents at Isengard, as it does not directly concern the paths we are considering in this book, but instead leave it for those who read The Lord of the Rings. But we will have much more to say about Saruman when we discuss the Path of the Wizard.

THE GREETERS AT ISENGARD

When Gandalf, Aragorn, Gimli and Legolas arrive at Isengard, along with King Théoden and his nephew and heir Éomer, and their army of men, they find Saruman's great fortress reduced to rubble. And as they look about they spot two small figures, totally at ease, surrounded by the remains of what must have been a very good meal. These small figures are, of course, Merry and Pippin in a typically insouciant pose. It is unlikely that a better picture of what Hobbits are like could be presented.

We'll talk about how Gandalf and company came to arrive at this meeting, and how Gandalf deals with Saruman in the chapter on the Path of the Wizard, but we need to mention another situation where Pippin lets his curiosity get the best of him: his encounter with the Palantir of Orthanc.

In the Elder Days, the Elf Fëanor of Noldor created seven Palantiri: "seeing-stones" made of crystal in the form of a globe. If someone of sufficient power gazed deeply into them, they could cast their mind wherever they wanted, without restrictions of time or space. Each stone had a different characteristic, an identity particular to it, yet all were linked together into a web, under the control of one stone, much like the Rings of Power. They were brought to Middle Earth in the Second Age where they were distributed and used by the Dúnedain, the men called the Elf-friends. Over time, however, some were lost and some passed into bad hands. Both Sauron and Saruman each had one, and as we will see later, so did Denethor, the Steward of Gondor. Saruman came under Sauron's control through the use of the Palantir he had acquired. After his defeat by the Ents , and his humiliation by Gandalf, Saruman's miserable lapdog Wormtongue (again of whom we will hear more later in our discussion of the Path of the King), not realizing its great worth, throws the Stone at Gandalf, to Gandalf's great delight. And ever-curious Pippin takes notice!

After taking center stage as the greeters to Isengard, Merry and Pippin fade into the background as first King Théoden, then Gandalf, confront Saruman. As a consequence, they once again feel small and unwanted. Pippin can't get Gandalf's reaction to the Palantir out of his mind. When he talks with Merry about it, Merry reminds him of a well-know aphorism: "*do not meddle in the affairs of wizards, for they are subtle and quick to anger.*"[26] But Pippin's curiosity refuses to be squelched. Once all are asleep, he creeps away and surreptitiously "borrows" the crystal ball from Gandalf's bedside. Once alone with the Palantir, "he bent low over it, looking like a greedy child stooping over a bowl of food."[27] Gazing into the crystal, he looks into the fiery eye of Sauron, where he is trapped. Sauron, expecting to see Saruman, asks who he is, and when he hears "a Hobbit," is delighted, thinking that Saruman has captured the Ring Bearer. But Sauron's power is so great that Pippin falls unconscious, thus preventing Sauron from learning the true situation.

When Gandalf discovers what has happened, upon reflection he decides that this mishap may have been providential. He himself might have looked into the Stone before he was ready to confront Sauron. And by chance—or fate?—Sauron has been misled into thinking himself closer to reacquiring his Ring than he actually is.

So the curiosity of the young Hobbit has caused trouble, but somehow it has also done good. This is a typical situation one encounters on the path of curiosity. When we are young, we all chafe at the bit and want to be treated like adults. We are impervious to the advice of our elders and insist that we are competent to deal with issues that are, at this point, beyond our capabilities. And so we act rashly and trouble results. But, hopefully, we learn from our failure. As Gandalf tells Pippin: "the burned hand teaches best. After that, advice about fire goes to the heart."[28]

PIPPIN AND MERRY PLEDGE THEIR ALLEGIANCE

To this point in the story, Merry and Pippin have been an inseparable pair, so much so that it is often hard to remember which words or actions belong to which character. Both have been overly fond of their comforts yet able to do without when needed; both have felt worthless and unwanted, homesick for the Shire, yet have continued the Quest. When captured by the Orcs, together they proved just how resourceful Hobbits can be. Afterwards, with Treebeard, their youth has been enough to rouse Treebeard from his long lethargy, to march on Isengard, and destroy Saruman's burgeoning empire. But ultimately we must each pick our own path, fight our own individual battles, find our unique destiny within the greater scheme of things. Merry and Pippin do just that. And, as if to prove they are like two halves of the same person, the paths they take are parallel.

Each now pledges his allegiance to a great man: Pippin to Denethor, the Steward of Gondor, father of Boromir and Faramir; Merry to King Théoden of Rohan, uncle of Éomer and Éowyn. Pippin makes the poorer choice. Impressed by the majesty of Denethor, and also nettled by Denethor's suspicion over the circumstances of his son Boromir's death, Pippin impulsively draws forth his small sword and lays it at Denethor's feet: "Little service, no doubt, will so great a lord of men think to find in a Hobbit, a halfling from the northern Shire; yet such as it is, I will offer it, in payment of my debt."[29] This gesture is enough to briefly bring out the best in Denethor, who graciously accepts Pippin's allegiance and keeps him by his side in Minis Tirith. Yet though Denethor looks to the outer eye much greater than Gandalf, even then Pippin senses that Gandalf is his superior in every way. He is to find out just how true this is as events progress.

Merry pledges his allegiance to a greater man than Denethor: King Théoden. In a touching speech, Merry says: "as a father you shall be to me," and Théoden, wise enough already to know his death approaches, responds "for a little while."[30]

Having chosen their individual paths, which leave them separated by many miles, both Merry and Pippin once again discover what little worth they seemingly have. In Gondor, the people are amazed at Pippin and regard him as the Prince of Halflings. But he feels less like a prince than a useless burden who has taken a silly path that has taken him away from his friends, especially Merry. Except for waiting on table for Denethor, Pippin has a great deal of time on his hands. He spends much of it with a warrior named Beregond, who shows him the ropes, and with Beregond's ten year old son Bergil. Because of Pippin's size, Bergil thinks Pippin a boy like himself, which amuses Pippin. But truly he has more fun playing with Bergil than he has had since separating from Merry.

Merry, in his turn, has been allowed to ride along with King Théoden as his Esquire, but the ride has proved long and weary and lonely without his friends, especially Pippin. But then, as if to show how much Merry has grown in emotional depth, he remembers Frodo and Sam, whose path is so much more difficult than any of theirs, and feels remorse.

A necessary part of growth is to realize that the world does not necessarily revolve around us, that others have their stories and that, perhaps, their stories might even be more important than ours in the greater scheme of things.

When it is finally time to go into battle, King Théoden tells Merry that he will have to leave him behind, as he and his warriors have to ride swiftly and Merry will only be an encumbrance. But Dernhelm, a strange rider with eyes of death, allows Merry to ride with him, hidden under his cloak. Of such small actions are great events made.

In Gondor, Pippin's great moment arrives. Seeing his remaining son Faramir lying in a near death state after being felled by a poisonous dart, Denethor goes mad and tries to immolate both himself and Faramir. Pippin persuades his new friend Beregond, who loves Faramir, to try and prevent the burning. Pippin runs to find Gandalf, and brings him back just in time to save Faramir. Cheated of his son, Denethor immolates himself, clutching his Palantir to his chest. It was this Palantir that led him to this sad state. In his arrogance he thought he was wise enough and powerful enough to use the Stone; instead, like Saruman, he fell prey to Sauron's lies and deceptions. And so he dies a sad death. But, as he dies, it's important to realize that, without Pippin's intervention, Faramir, a greater man than either his father Denethor or his brother Boromir, would have died.

Just as Merry chose the greater man to follow, Merry's accomplishment is the greater. In the epic Battle of the Pelennor Fields, the men of Rohan, led by their King, are defeating the massed forces of the Enemy outside the city of Gondor. But then a dart from the sky slays the King's great steed Snowmane, and the Lord of the Nazgûls, riding on a monstrous flying creature, swoops down upon the King. One warrior stands between the Black Rider and his prey: the strange warrior Dernhelm. At that moment Dernhelm reveals herself to be the King's niece, the warrior princess Éowyn. She takes advantage of this moment of surprise to cut off the head of the Nazgûl's flying steed. But then the Black Rider's mace shatters her shield, crushing her shoulder, and she falls stunned to the ground.

And, at the moment of truth, Merry reveals himself to be as great as any warrior in *The Lord of the Rings*. Lying on the ground, cowering in fear, he cries out Éowyn's name, then raises his tiny sword and stabs the Lord of the Nazgûls in his leg. As the Black Rider sinks to the ground, Éowyn, with her final action, stabs him in the empty space where his face should be. Her sword shatters and she falls upon her foe. But when she does, there's nothing left but an empty cloak and chain mail, and a terrible wail that fades away, leaving no further trace of the Lord of the Nazgûls to trouble the world.

King Théoden raises his head. Unaware of what has transpired, he is able to die happy, thinking that he has killed the Lord of the Nazgûls. Merry weeps for the King and for Éowyn, who lies as if dead. His arm is numb and he watches his sword, the sword that pierced the Black Rider, smoke, then wither away into dust. He has no idea that this sword, which was acquired from the Barrow-downs in the first days after leaving the Shire, was a work of Westernesse, and that only such a blade could have cut the binding spells that gave body to the Black Rider.

When Éomer arrives with his men and finds both the King and, seemingly, his sister dead, he orders the bodies to be borne away in state, then turns back to the battle, to fight as someone does who has noone left on earth whom he loves. As his men bear Théoden and Éowyn away, Merry trudges along behind them, as unaware of his surroundings as the men are unaware of his great role in this pivotal event.

When he reaches the city and Pippin greets him, it's more than Merry can take and he begins weeping: for the King and Éowyn, and perhaps without knowing it, for his own loss of innocence in his confrontation with a living symbol of darkness. When a little later Pippin stands at Merry's bedside, he fears that Merry will die. But Aragorn has healed his wound (we will discuss Aragorn as Healer in the chapter on the Path of the King), and reassures Pippin that, though Merry has been deeply hurt by his contact with the Lord of the Nazgûls, he will survive. "So strong and gay a spirit is in him. His grief he will not forget; but it will not darken his heart, it will teach him wisdom."[31]

Both Merry and Pippin have had to learn wisdom the hard way, through facing darkness, which is perhaps the only way it can be learned.

RETURN TO THE SHIRE FOR THE BATTLE OF BYWATER

Merry and Pippin have now played their roles in the Quest for the Ring. It remains for Kings and Warriors and Dwarves and Elves, and most of all, Frodo and Sam, to complete the Quest. But the story doesn't end after Frodo has saved Middle Earth, and the new King has been crowned and wed to his Queen, as all other such stories do.

In this story, we follow the Hobbits back to their home in the Shire. On the way, they stop at the *Inn of the Prancing Pony*, as they did on their way to begin their journey. This time, rather than playing the fool for the others staying at the inn, they find themselves regarded with amazement and not a little fear because of their battle gear. They are by this time so used to the apparel of war that they don't even realize how unusual they look to more peaceful folk. While they were fighting a war, those back home have suffered at the fringes of the war, without knowing what was taking place. As they leave, the innkeeper Butterbur tells them that they look like warriors who can deal with any sort of trouble they might encounter. And when Merry tells Gandalf that he's sure he will take care of things, Gandalf tells him that he won't be returning with them to the Shire. They're all grown up now and can handle their own problems. They have become much greater than they realize and have no need for wizards like him.

Moral growth occurs so gradually that we are the last to recognize greatness in ourselves.

And so they find out! The Shire has been taken over by men: thugs who have co-opted the Hobbits pitiful equivalent of a police force, using the Hobbits to do their dirty work for them, much as the Nazis used the French Vichy government during WWII. There are new rules and laws against seemingly everything, even their beloved pipeweed. Merry and Pippin and Frodo and Sam don't even bother to confront the puppet Hobbits, simply ignoring their rules and forcing the police to follow behind them, pretending that they are under guard. And when they are eventually confronted by a small number of men, their appearance, their swords, and especially their confidence, are enough to send the men scurrying away.

But it is clear that the hoodlums won't give up that easily. By this time, Frodo has done his great deed and stands above the strife, much like a Gandhi, desiring only peace. But Merry and Pippin have learned the warrior's role and so take charge. They organize the Hobbits of the Shire and the last great battle of Hobbit history takes place: the Battle of Bywater. Seventy of the evil men die and a dozen are taken prisoner, while the Hobbits suffer nineteen dead and thirty more to injury. But they have regained the Shire for all time. Led by Merry and Pippin, the two little Hobbits who seemed so inconsequential as the story began!

In the years that follow Merry, now called the Magnificent by other Hobbits, becomes Master of Buckland. Pippin becomes the Took (the leader of the Took clan) and the Thain (the Chief Executive of the Shire, whose power begins where the Mayor's ends). He is also the physically largest Hobbit in memory (undoubtedly due to the Ent draughts). In old age, Merry is asked to visit his old friend King Éomer of Rohan one last time, and is at his side when he dies. Pippin then rejoins Merry and they travel to Gondor, where they spend their last days, and are buried among the great of Gondor.

Thus ends the Path of Curiosity, a path that might guide many, if not all, of us.

Chapter Two
The Path of Opposites

In some way, all growth involves the reconciliation between opposites. As humans, we are constantly pulled between body and mind, instinct and spirit, that which connects us to the earth, and that which connects us to the universe. We are both animal and god stuffed into one uncomfortable package. In *The Lord of the Rings*, we see that contrast drawn most clearly between two characters who each represent one side of that polarity: Gimli the Dwarf, and Legolas the Elf. Gimli is short and squat and powerful, each step so solid he seems almost rooted in the earth. Legolas is tall and fair and seems to float over the earth as he moves. Earth and air, instinct and spirit. If they can find common ground, *we* can find that common ground inside ourselves.

FIRST MEETINGS

We first meet Legolas at the Council of Elrond in Rivendell, where the Fellowship is formed. After Gandalf tells the story of the Ring and Gollum's part in it, Legolas reveals the bad news that Gollum has escaped from the Elves. When Aragorn wonders how the Elves could have failed in such an important responsibility, Legolas says that it wasn't that they didn't watch him closely, but that they couldn't bear to keep him forever shut up in dungeons beneath the earth (which we should note is exactly where Dwarves, in contrast, choose to live). Gimli's father Glóin, who had himself once been imprisoned by the Elves, immediately reacts with anger, saying "you were less tender to me."[32] Gandalf is forced to remind them that they have to set aside past differences between Dwarves and Elves in order to fight a common enemy.

So we immediately see the opposition between Dwarves and Elves. Within our own personalities, we often feel an opposition between our conscious personality, the person who we think we are, and our unconscious personality, which carries shadow qualities that we reject in ourselves. Someone with a bigger perspective could see that those shadow qualities complement the traits we acknowledge, and that the union of both is what we need for a fully three-dimensional personality.

Soon after the company is formed, we see the contrast between Gimli and Legolas even in their battle gear. Gimli wears a heavy vest of steel rings, and carries a large axe for a weapon. Solid and heavy. Legolas wears no armor and carries only a knife, bow and arrows. Light and airy. Over the course of their many battles together, we see just how well both can use these characteristic weapons.

Just before the fellowship of the Ring leave, Elrond tells them that they are free to leave the quest at any point. When Gimli responds firmly that "faithless is he that says farewell when the road darkens,"[33] we get the feeling that when Gimli says something, his word is as solid and substantial as is Gimli himself. Gimli will never fail in his commitment, no matter what happens along the way.

CARADHRAS THE CRUEL

Two weeks out from Rivendell on their quest, the company sees the mountains in the near distance, which confuses Pippin. When Gandalf teases Pippin that he probably never looked at the maps in Elrond's house, Gimli interjects that he doesn't need any map to know the land of his forefathers. The art and music and literature of the Dwarves are filled with images of these mountains. "They stand tall in our dreams."[34] As he continues, he eloquently names each of the mountains, and the love of his race for them shines through his words. Though one mountain's name sounds less than lovely: "Caradhras the Cruel." And it is through the Redhorn Gate, a pass next to Caradhras, that they must travel.

Perhaps we might see Dwarves as the engineers of their world. Nothing airy-fairy for Dwarves: they deal with solid things like metal and stone. But they make something beautiful out of those solid objects. Though rooted in the earth, they also create songs and tales, and they dream!

But when they arrive at Caradhras, hoping to get across before the first snow of winter, snow starts falling immediately, as if the mountain was aware of their presence and resented it. As the snow drifts mount, the way becomes increasingly difficult, until both Gimli and the Hobbits are barely able to move. When Boromir boasts that "the strongest of us must seek a way,"[35] he and Aragorn struggle mightily, trying to force a path for the others through the snow. Legolas smiles at their futile effort and says: "the strongest must seek a way, say you? But I say: let a ploughman plough, but choose an otter for swimming, and for running light over grass and leaf, or over snow—an elf."[36] He then runs on top of the snow as easily as if it were hard ground, and is soon lost to their sight, as he seeks for some place of refuge for the company. Frodo notices that Legolas doesn't bother to wear boots like the rest of the company, simply light shoes. After an hour, he returns, running as lightly as ever, to say that he was able to find a place where the snow drifts, while high, are not very deep, so that Aragorn and Boromir can force a pathway down the mountain for the others.

We begin to see more of the contrast between Dwarves and Elves. Where Dwarves are solid and stable, bound to the Earth, the natural element of Elves is the Air. They move so lightly that they leave not a mark running over snow. Though we need solidity and stability in our daily life, there comes a time in all our lives when we become too solid, too stable, and threaten to sink beneath the weight of our hard-won identity with its mundane responsibilities. At such times, we need a light, airy part that can float above the day-to-day minutia, that can get us past our stuck place, in order to see what lies beyond. We need both Gimli and Legolas—stability and imagination.

THE MINES OF MORIA

Defeated by Caradhras, the company is now forced to go through the mines of Moria. Though the mere mention of the name brings fear to all (including Gandalf and Aragorn, who are the only ones who have actually passed through the mines), these caves have no fear for Gimli. For him, Moria represents the peak of the Dwarves' achievements, and he is eager to find if there are still Dwarves living there in splendor.

Legolas the Elf is hardly as enthusiastic, and says simply that he doesn't want to go there. But it is Frodo who is the Ring bearer and Frodo who decides that this is the path they must take.

None of us want to go deep into the darkness that lies within us, but sometimes we arrive at a point when this is the only way to progress. We can't move any further without finding out who we really are and who we are intended to be. And that inevitably means going into the darkness inside our soul.

When they arrive at the gate, Gandalf explains that the West-door was made in a time when there was friendship between all races, even Dwarves and Elves. Gimli immediately insists that it wasn't the Dwarves that caused the friendship to end. And Legolas responds that it certainly wasn't the Elves' fault. And again Gandalf has to remind them that they need to remain friends on the journey, as they are both needed.

In the early stages of reconciling the opposites, there is often more quarreling than peace. It is difficult for either side to appreciate its opposite.

Meanwhile, Gandalf struggles to find the right magic word to open the gate. The directions seemed simple enough: "speak, friend, and enter."[37] But Gandalf tries every magical password he knows and the gate remains unmoved. Finally, a thought occurs to him and with a laugh he says simply "friend" in Elvish and the doors open. Truly this was in a simpler time when the races of Elves and Dwarves and men trusted one another.

Sometimes we reach a place where we can't seem to find an opening, a doorway. We exhaust all our conscious resources and, when we are tired enough to give up that struggle, we find that the answer is right before our eyes.

Once inside the caves, everyone but Gimli is unpleasantly overwhelmed, feeling as if they were suddenly reduced to ants inside a giant ant hill, an ant hill filled with endless corridors branching into enormous halls, each so high that the ceilings fade from sight. Nothing they had ever heard could match the fearful majesty of Moria. Still, Gimli's presence, along with Gandalf and Aragorn's leadership, gives courage to his companions. But even Gimli finds that the Mines of Moria are far too intricate for him to do little more than follow along with the others behind Gandalf's lead.

Only someone who has passed through the darkness within their own personality can really guide us. Such people are often termed "wounded healers" because in dealing with their own inner wounds, they acquire the wisdom to heal others.

When Sam wonders how anyone could have created all these corridors, and why they would want to live in such "darksome holes,"[38] Gimli defends his ancestors, insisting that Moria was the greatest achievement of the Dwarves. In its heyday it was "full of light and splendour."[39] Then he chants an ancient song about these halls as they were in the days when Durin, the great founder of the Dwarf race, lived.

We don't have to fear the darkness within us. It is quite possible to shed light on it and see it as lovely and splendid.

But that was long ago. As they proceed further, they come to a chamber holding a large tomb, the tomb of Balin—the last Dwarf leader to return to Moria. At this discovery, Gimli hides his face so that the others won't see his distress. Gandalf finds a journal left behind by the Dwarves and reads out loud of the last days of the Dwarves, slain either by Orcs or by something worse. Toward the end of the journal the writer says "We cannot get out. we cannot get out." And "they are coming."

From time immemorial, we all come to a place where we feel under siege and we cannot get out. So it was in ancient times and so it is today.

As Gandalf finishes reading, the company hears the sounds of horns and drums and running feet coming toward them. Unconsciously repeating the words of the journal, Legolas cries "They are coming!" and Gimli adds that "we cannot get out."[40] Onset by Orcs, we see for the first time that both Gimli with his axe, and Legolas with his bow and arrow, are truly fearsome warriors. But then something much worse that Orcs appears, a creature of some earlier, viler time: a Balrog! But the story of how Gandalf's self-sacrifice enables the company to escape from the Balrog is better left for the chapter on the Path of Wizards.

LOTHLÓRIEN & GALADRIEL

From the dark gloom of the Mines of Moria our heroes come to the shining light of Lothlórien, the Elven kingdom ruled by Lord Celeborn and Lady Galadriel. As they enter Lothlórien, Legolas tells his companions tales of this forest kingdom, still remembered by his fellow Elves in Mirkwood. At the musical sound of a nearby waterfall, Legolas explains that it is named after the legendary Elven maiden Nimrodel. He sings her story, a tale of love found and lost, then finds himself stopping in sadness. He says that this is only part of a much longer tale, much of which he has forgotten: "it tells how sorrow came upon Lothlórien, Lórien of the Blossom, when the Dwarves awakened evil in the Mountains."[41] When Gimli reminds him that "the dwarves did not make the evil,"[42] Legolas grants him that, a small sign that perhaps their antagonism is becoming somewhat more muted.

Soon afterwards, the party is captured by wood Elves, who come upon them so silently that even Legolas is taken by surprise. Legolas explains who he and his companions are, and asks for a place to rest on their journey. The Elves have no trouble with anyone except Gimli—the idea of a Dwarf in Lothlórien is repellant to them. But when Legolas reminds them that Gimli was selected by Elrond himself, they reluctantly agree that he can come, too, but only if guarded by Aragorn and Legolas. They proceed deeper into the forest, but when they come to the Naith of Lórien, its inner core, the Elves insist that Gimli must be blindfolded. When Gimli bristles at this and grasps his axe, Legolas complains "a plague on dwarves and their stiff necks!"[43]

Aragorn resolves the problem by insisting that, if Gimli must blindfolded, then the whole company must be as well. While Gimli finds this solution humorous and says that he'll be satisfied if only Legolas is blindfolded, it's Legolas' turn to bristle; he doesn't see the humor in having to be treated like a prisoner by his fellow Elves. But Legolas gives way and the whole company enters the Naith blindfolded.

Though this scene provides humor and shows how uneasy the relationship still is between Legolas and Gimli, there is a hidden meaning as well. In order to enter the holiest places, we must be "blindfolded;" i.e., cut off from our normal sensory view of reality, so that we can open our eyes to deeper meanings that lie beneath the surface. Only by doing that can we find an inner guide like Galadriel.

When finally they are brought before Celeborn and Galadriel, Celeborn greets each of them by name, clearly already knowing who they are and why they have come. Unlike the Elves who captured the company, he is as courteous to Gimli as to the rest of his companions, and expresses the hope that his arrival, together with the Elves' willingness to break old rules and welcome him, marks the beginning of a new friendship between Elves and Dwarves. Gimli bows graciously in response to his kind words, but it is when Galadriel looks at him and smiles that his life is forever transformed. He looks up and sees her sweet smile, and hears her speaking in the ancient Dwarf tongue, which falls from her lips as if she were born to it. Instead of enmity and hatred he feels love and understanding. Something melts inside Gimli. He smiles back, bows, and looking into her eyes, says that "the Lady Galadriel is above all the jewels that lie beneath the earth."[44]

It is hard to overstate the importance of Galadriel's impact on the company. As we will see in other chapters dealing with other paths, because Galadriel is able to see into the deepest part of each person's soul, each is affected in a different way. For some, Boromir in particular, this is a source of deep discomfort. For Gimli, it is a revelation, because Galadriel is able to see past his gruff exterior to his pure heart. It is significant that he feels loved by this apotheosis of the feminine. To this point in the story, we see only masculine values in Gimli: courage and pride, steadfastness and loyalty, but no tenderness or empathy, and certainly no love. Galadriel changes all that and makes it possible for Gimli and Legolas to find a friendship that bridges their differences.

This is equally true within ourselves. The opposition between the person we have come to believe ourselves to be, and the shadow within that is equally us, can only be overcome through a gentle, feminine touch. It is only the feminine that can fully reconcile inner oppositions. Often we experience this through tears that come to melt away the hard places inside us, to create a "solution" in which all the essential parts remain, but now ready to be recombined into someone new. The resolution is neither the person who we already think ourselves to be, or the person inside that we reject, but someone new who is a combination of both.

After receiving the rest and succor they need, the time comes for the company to continue on their quest. The Elves give each of them *lembas*, elven wafers of bread that are able to provide more energy than any human food. Each also receives a hooded cloak made of a wondrously light material that blends with their surroundings to form camouflage. Each cloak is held at the neck by a green and silver brooch (a brooch that Pippin treasures yet later sacrifices, hoping—rightly—that Aragorn will find it). They are given three small grey boats to take them down the great river Silverlode (also known as Celebrant). In each boat are coils of light yet almost miraculously strong rope (which will come in handy for Sam and Frodo more than once in the times to come).

Each also receives a personal gift from Galadriel. For Aragorn, a beautiful sheath made perfectly to fit his famed sword Andúril, as well as the Elfstone of the house of Elendil, to mark him as the rightful king of Gondor. There is a belt of gold for Boromir, silver belts for Merry and Pippin. Legolas receives a very practical gift: a new bow and quiver of arrows. Sam receives a very great gift: a tiny plain wooden box containing earth taken from Galadriel's own garden which she has blessed. Only near the end of *The Lord of the Rings* do we learn the full powers of this earth. Frodo receives a crystal phial in which "is caught the light of Eärendil's star,"[45] a light that will shine when all other lights fail.

But when Galadriel turns to Gimli and asks gently what gift he would have from her, he tells her none at all, for the mere sight of her and the sound of her words has been sufficient gift for him. Galadriel is clearly touched and begs him to ask something of her. Timidly Gimli asks if he might have a single strand of her golden hair "which surpasses the gold of the earth as the stars surpass the gems of the mine."[46] Everyone but Galadriel is taken aback by this; she merely smiles and asks what he would do with this strange gift. Gimli says that he would treasure it, and if he survives he would take it home and have it set in crystal as a sign of goodwill between Elves and Dwarves. At that, Galadriel cuts three long golden hairs and gives them to him, saying that "your hands shall flow with gold, and yet over you gold shall have no dominion."[47]

Though none of the company will ever forget Galadriel, none will sing her praises higher than Gimli! As the company rides away down the river, Gimli—this hard-bitten Dwarf who have never previously shown any soft emotion—openly weeps. He tells Legolas he had no idea when he began this quest that the greatest danger would be seeing such beauty, then having to leave it, probably forever. Legolas, touched, tells him that he is a brave and true companion and he will always have this memory in his heart. Gimli thanks Legolas for his kind words, but tells him that memory is different for Dwarves and Elves. While Elves can live in a memory as if it were reality, for Dwarves (as for men) a memory is only a mirror reflecting reality, As they pass out of sight of Lothlórien, their joint experience of Galadriel has made them fast friends forever.

CHASING THE ORCS

In the previous chapter on Merry and Pippin, we described Boromir's treachery, redemption, and death. With Frodo and Sam off on their lonely quest, Merry and Pippin captured by the Orcs, and Gandalf seemingly dead, all that is left of the original company are Aragorn, Gimli and Legolas. They consider the situation and decide that their best course of action is to chase the Orcs in order to try and rescue Merry and Pippin. The Orcs have quite a head-start and Aragorn points out that Orcs move swiftly and don't tire. When Gimli answers proudly that "dwarves too can go swiftly, and they do not tire sooner than Orcs," Aragorn replies that "we shall all need the endurance of dwarves."[48]

Once on their way, we find that Legolas has skills that surpass both Gimli and Aragorn. At one point he spots an eagle high in the sky, far beyond even Aragorn's keen eyes. Time and again throughout the rest of the tale, Legolas' incredible Elf vision will be demonstrated. And, despite Gimli's proud claim, Legolas proves to have an inhuman endurance that exceeds that of both Dwarves and men. After running from dusk of the first day, through the night, then on through the day to the next dusk, with only brief rests on their way, Aragorn calls a halt, both because Gimli is exhausted and for fear of losing the trail at night. Legolas, seemingly tireless, would go on, but agrees that the others need rest. Gimli and Aragorn drop to the ground and fall asleep almost instantly.

When Aragorn wakes before dawn, he sees Legolas standing, looking off in the distance. The two wake Gimli, then again run all the next day, bolstered only by the Elven lembas which they can eat on the run for energy. As before, they are forced to stop at darkness from the weariness of Man and Dwarf. Again when they wake in the morning, Legolas is already up, if he has ever slept at all.

As they run for still another day, both Gimli and Aragorn are weighed down both from the effort of the chase and from their fear that they are too late to save their friends. Only Legolas remains unchanged, still running so lightly that no mark of his passing is left on the earth. As he runs, his consciousness is split between his outer surroundings and his inner world. That timeless dream-like world of the Elves sustains him as sleep refreshes his comrades. That night, Aragorn and Gimli sleep restlessly. Whenever they wake briefly in the night, they see Legolas either standing nearby or walking back and forth, singing softly to himself.

We saw earlier that the company had to be blindfolded in order to enter the holiest core of the Elven realm. We can only see the inner world with "inner eyes." But eventually we have to come out once more into the mundane world and view the world with our normal senses. The rules for the two worlds are as different as are Legolas and Gimli. The ultimate goal is to be so comfortable in both inner and outer worlds that we learn, like Legolas, how to live in both worlds at the same time.

As Joseph Campbell says: "Freedom to pass back and forth across the world division, from the perspective of the apparitions of time to that of the causal deep and back—not contaminating the principles of the one with those of the other, yet permitting the mind to know the one by virtue of the other—is the talent of the master."[49]

THE RIDERS OF ROHAN AND THE REAPPEARANCE OF GANDALF

We again see proof of Legolas' remarkable vision when Aragorn spots riders approaching on the horizon. Legolas notes their exact number, the yellow color of their hair, the brightness of their spears, and the fact that their leader is tall. When Aragorn smiles and remarks "Keen are the eye of the elves," Legolas demurs and says that they're only five leagues away [about 3 miles!].

Éomer, the leader of the riders of Rohan, asks them to identify themselves and explain their purpose. When Aragorn mentions that they have come most recently from Lothlórien, Éomer makes a disparaging remark about the feared "Lady in the Golden Wood." Gimli will have none of that and tells him that "you speak evil of that which is far beyond the reach of your thought, and only little wit can excuse you."[50] When Éomer prepares to fight, Legolas immediately draws his bow, telling Éomer that he would die before he could touch Gimli. Clearly Legolas and Gimli are now friends to the death. While everyone pauses in shock to see an Elf defending a Dwarf, Aragorn mends the situation with soothing words.

After things calm down, and Aragorn explains more of their mission to save their friends. Éomer is stunned to hear that they have run 45 leagues [about 135 miles] in less than four days, and tells Aragorn that his name should be Wingfoot, not Strider. Éomer then describes his men's battle with Orcs, but says that they saw no such creatures as the Hobbits described by Aragorn. The reader knows that this is because Merry and Pippin have managed to escape and are already on their way to meeting Treebeard.

Now that peace is restored, Éomer agrees to give them horses, but one of this followers argues against loaning one to a Dwarf. Gimli, as usual, bristles at this and insists he would rather walk. But this time, rather than cursing the stiff back of Dwarves, Legolas solves the problem by suggesting that Gimli ride behind him, so he won't have to borrow a horse. From this point on, the two are inseparable, joined in friendship much like Merry and Pippin, with both the implicit trust and the friendly teasing that goes with such a relationship. But in this case, it is a joining of opposites, not similarities.

Later that night, after leaving the company and, for a change, riding instead of running, a strange old man appears mysteriously then disappears again just as mysteriously. In the process, their horses run away. When Gimli complains at the loss of their horses, Legolas teases him that only a few hours before he didn't even want to sit on a horse. The three try to sort out who or what the old man was, and why the horses ran away, without reaching any firm conclusions.

The next day, they continue on, once more on foot, until they come to the site of the battle between the Orcs and the riders of Rohan. As they move outward from the battle site, looking for traces of Merry and Pippin, Aragorn finds both pieces of cut cord and a mallorn-leaf from Loth Lórien with crumbs of lembas on it. When Gimli spots the Orc knife that cut the cord, Aragorn interprets the evidence to mean that one of the Hobbits was carried to this spot by an Orc, who was later killed by the riders, and his body dragged away. The Hobbit managed to use the Orc's discarded knife to cut his bonds, then sat and ate the Elven waybread. Aragorn also realizes why the Orcs were content to take Merry and Pippin after Boromir was killed, rather than continuing the hunt for Frodo: they must have thought that one of the two Hobbits was the Ringbearer wanted by Sauron.

The mood of the trio lightens immeasurably, now that they know that at least one of the young Hobbits is still alive. Continuing their search for signs, they discover light footprints of Hobbits, whether one or two is impossible to judge, leading into the dread forest of Fangorn. As they enter the forest, Gimli immediately senses evil. To Legolas, more sensitive to the moods of trees, the feeling is not evil, but watchful and angry, an anger caused by suffering. He tells the other two that the forest is so old that "almost I feel young again, as I have not felt since I journeyed with you children."[51] He says he could have been happy in Fangorn if he had come there in a different time.

By this point, after seeing Legolas' more than human (or Dwarf) abilities and endurance on their unbelievable run, we begin to fully appreciate that Elves are a race apart from the others: immortal beings who neither tire nor die. Legolas' quiet reference to Aragorn and Gimli as "children" emphasizes just how ancient Elves are, and how tiny are the life spans of even long-lived Dwarves or Dúnedain like Aragorn, in comparison with that of Elves. Though living by choice in Middle Earth for thousands of years, the Elves clearly regard this time as but a sojourn. We need to recognize that there is such an indestructible, immortal part in each of us. The difficulty in life is to find an accommodation between that transpersonal element and our all too mortal self. But if two so opposite as Gimli and Legolas can form an indissoluble bond, it is possible for all.

Soon afterwards, they once again see the mysterious old man, who reveals himself to be Gandalf. The horses were called away by his steed, the great Shadowfax. The story of how Gandalf survived the Balrog and was transformed from Gandalf the Grey into Gandalf the White will be told in our next chapter: the Path of Wizards. After everyone shares their adventures, Gandalf takes his friends with him to Rohan, where he persuades King Théoden to rise from his doldrums and help defeat the forces of Sauron. Again that story must be deferred.

THEIR "COMPETITION" IN BATTLE

We return to our tale of Legolas and Gimli at the point when King Théoden is ready to lead his men in defense against the forces of Isengard. Gimli impatiently tells Legolas "well, at last we set off! Men need many words before deeds."[52] At the gate of the city, when Éomer approaches, Gimli is somewhat ill-at-ease after their quarrel over Galadriel at their previous meeting. But he is mollified when Éomer asks him to put aside their quarrel, and promises to speak no ill of Galadriel. Gimli somewhat teasingly says he will, but if Éomer ever sees Galadriel, he must then acknowledge her the fairest of all ladies, or suffer Gimli's wrath. With the quarrel fully mended, Éomer graciously offers Gimli a ride on his horse. Gimli gladly accepts, provided only that Legolas rides next to them. Remember, the two are now inseparable. Legolas then takes his place to Éomer's left, Aragorn to his right as they ride off.

The company rides five hours until darkness falls, then rise at dawn to ride again. They finally come upon one of the soldiers who had been left to defend against the forces of Sauron. At first, he is overcome at the sight of Théoden restored to vigor and leading his men, but then tells them that the enemy now include not only Orcs, but also the wild hillmen of the area. The defenders have been overrun; those who remain alive have retreated to Helm's Gate, a fortress at the mouth of the caves of Helm's Deep, where most of the old and the young and the women of the area have fled.

By that night, Théoden's men have joined the forces at Helm's Gate. On the parapet of Helm's Gate, Gimli is finally in his element, with firm stone beneath him, while Legolas feels ill at ease. The contrast with their relative reactions to Fangorn is marked. But Legolas adds that at least he feels better having Gimli there beside him.

The enemy doesn't wait for dawn, attacking soon after midnight. Once the battle has begun, we see just what magnificent warriors both Legolas and Gimli are. They even begin a friendly, though grisly, competition to see who can kill the most Orcs. This competition will go back and forth throughout the battle. Initially Gimli kills two Orcs with his ax, but his triumph is short-lived when he discovers Legolas has already killed twenty with his bow and arrows. After more fighting, Gimli announces proudly that he's up to twenty-one, but now finds that Legolas has been involved in hand-to-hand fighting with his knife and his total is now up to two dozen.

The two friends are separated during the course of the battle, and Legolas is worried when he finds out from Aragorn that Gimli is nowhere to be found. In the typically low-key manner that all the heros deal with worry, however, he tells Aragorn he wanted to tell Gimli that his count was up to thirty-nine. When, at the end of the battle, Gimli emerges from the caves beneath Helm's Deep with a head-band stained with blood, the first thing he tells Legolas is that his score is up to forty-two. Legolas tells him that forty-two beats his total by one, but that he is so happy to see him, that he doesn't mind being beaten. This is the way warriors profess their love for each other. The two friends are never again apart.

THE BARGAIN

When Gandalf is ready to ride on to Isengard with Aragorn and Legolas, Gimli refuses to stay behind, discounting his wound as a mere "Orc-scratch." Legolas and Gimli ride together on one horse, once more inseparable companions. Passing through Fangorn, even Legolas is uneasy with the level of anger he feels in the forest. They are not yet aware that the Ents have gone on their great march to Isengard, raising the emotions of the trees as they passed.

As they ride, Gimli eloquently tells Legolas of the beauties of Helm's Deep. They make a bargain that when all is over, Gimli will visit Fangorn with Legolas, and Legolas will see Helm's Deep. In other words, so deep is their friendship now, they each are willing to go into the place that makes them feel the most uncomfortable, simply because their friend values it. And in fact, once in Isengard, Legolas persuades Treebeard to let Gimli visit Fangorn with him later - even though Dwarves and their axes are not normally welcome there.

THROUGH THE PATHS OF THE DEAD TO MINIS TIRITH

After their reunion with Merry and Pippin at Isengard, their next challenge is to accompany Aragorn and his men, the Rangers, through the Paths of the Dead. It is both the shortest route toward the East where they must meet the forces of Sauron, and also the path Aragorn must take in order to fulfill his destiny. We will say more on this in the chapter on the Path of the King. As they enter the Haunted Mountain through the Gate of the Dead, even Gimli, a Dwarf who normally loves caves, is frightened. "The company halted, and there was not a heart among them that did not quail, unless it were the heart of Legolas of the Elves, for whom the ghosts of Men have no terror."[53] When their horse refuses to enter the cave, Legolas covers the horse's eyes, sings some words in his ear, and then leads him in. Gimli stands in terror, angry at himself, then says: "Here is a thing unheard of! An elf will go underground and a dwarf will not!"[54] Then he forces himself to enter at the rear of the company, where he can see the ghosts of ancient warriors rising from their graves to follow them. As they move onwards, his fear grows stronger, since he alone knows that they can't turn back, not with the dead behind.

Of course, those who, like Legolas, have no fear, can also never learn to master fear, since they have none. It is in passing through the Paths of the Dead that we truly see just how brave Gimli is. The inner world, which is beyond life and death, is indeed frightening for the living. But we must all face death inside ourselves and come out the other side.

But they do make it through the Paths of the Dead and engage in one last battle together, the Battle of Pellenor Fields outside Minis Tirith. There is no description in the book of their roles in this battle. Perhaps any such description would be anti-climactic after their competition at Helm's Gate. But the morning after the Battle, when Legolas and Gimli enter Minis Tirith, the people of the city are amazed to see such a pair walking together: Legolas, who like all Elves has more than human beauty and grace, and Gimli, short and squat, who only another Dwarf (or Galadriel) could see as beautiful.

Gimli's characteristic reaction to Minis Tirith is that the masonry isn't bad, but it could be improved by Dwarves. Legolas' equally characteristic rejoinder is that they need more greenery to make their hearts happy. Both decide to make suggestions to Aragorn for improvements when he becomes king. In fact, before they leave, Aragorn vows that if they finally triumph, he will ask Gimli to lead the Dwarves in rebuilding the great gate outside Minis Tirith, which was destroyed in the battle. Which he later does. And Aragorn will plant a new tree in the court of the kingdom and the kingdom will become once more green and lovely. But now, Legolas and Gimli continue to talk as friends do in the brief quiet times between battles, debating back and forth whether "the deeds of Men will outlast us, Gimli," as Legolas says, or whether ultimately men will "come to naught in the end but might-have-beens,"[55] as Gimli argues. When Legolas sees sea gulls in the distance, he feels the "sea-longing" inside him, the desire to go back to the Havens, the Elven home over the sea. Gimli doesn't want to lose his friend and tries to persuade him that there is still much to see in Middle-Earth and it would be a poorer place without Elves.

Again we see that there is a need for both: for good, solid stone work and for lovely growing gardens. There is a need to return to the place of the spirit over the sea, and a need to stay in the mortal world as long as possible.

THE HAVENS

After Sauron's defeat and Aragorn's coronation and then marriage to Arwen Evenstar, Éomer and Gimli have a final debate over Galadriel's merits. When Éomer tells Gimli that now that he has seen Galadriel, he can still not say that she is the fairest of all, Gimli, goes for his axe, though now largely in jest. After Éomer pleads that the only reason he does not choose Galadriel is because he has seen Queen Arwen Evenstar, Gimli excuses him, saying "you have chosen the Evening, but my love is given to the Morning. And my heart forebodes that soon it will pass away forever."[56] For he knows that with the passing of Sauron also comes the time when the Elves will soon return to their home over the Sea.

And, in fact, Galadriel and the other Elves do soon pass over the Sea. Save only Arwen, who has chosen to live as a mortal with her husband Aragorn, and Legolas, who still needs to spend time in Middle-Earth with his new friend. And he does remain for a good time by human reckoning. They travel together and visit both the caves of Helm's Deep and the forest Fangorn. But when, in the course of time, the long-lived Aragorn finally dies, Legolas knows that it is time to return to his home beyond the sea.

But something unprecedented takes place—Legolas takes Gimli with him to the Undying lands! Never before has a Dwarf desired this journey, nor have the Elven lords ever before permitted it. "But it may be said that Gimli went also out of desire to see again the beauty of Galadriel; and it may be that she, mighty among the Eldar, obtained this grace for him. More cannot be said of this matter."[57]

Certainly I'll say nothing more.

Chapter Three
The Path of the Wizard

We've seen in chapter one, in our discussion of Merry and Pippin, how their youthful curiosity drew them out from the safe comfort of the Shire into the wonders and dangers of the greater world. Though they were often frightened and homesick, they fought the battles they needed to fight with courage and humility, and came home much greater than when they left. In chapter two, in our discussion of Legolas and Gimli, we saw how, beginning with enmity, each found first accommodation, then friendship, then something approaching love for their opposite. But there are levels beyond each of these paths, and we now come to one: the Path of the Wizard, the path of the wise. And we will see that even for the wisest, life has mysteries and dangers and hurdles that have to be overcome.

We first encounter Gandalf in *The Hobbit*, but that lighter story does not concern us here, except as it starts the process in motion that eventually leads to the quest for the Ring. Among his many adventures with Gandalf and the Dwarves in killing the dragon Smaug and stealing his treasure, Bilbo also steals the One Ring (though no one at this point knows it to be that) from Gollum. But, just as Gollum killed to acquire the Ring, yet called it his birthday present, so too does Bilbo lie and claim that it was a gift from Gollum after Bilbo solved Gollum's riddle. In the prologue of *The Lord of the Rings*, we find, however, that Gandalf doesn't believe Bilbo's story for one moment. But since even wise Gandalf does not yet know the Ring's true significance, he turns to other matters, and over fifty years go by before we again meet Gandalf at Bilbo's one-hundred-eleventh birthday party, where the story of the Ring resumes.

FIREWORKS & COUNSEL

Hobbits have a special fascination for Gandalf and he has visited the Shire many times in the past. To the Hobbits, he seems a somewhat doddering old geezer, and is largely known for the wonderful fireworks that he displays at special events. When he arrives for Bilbo's birthday party, everyone looks forward to seeing his skills in action, and he doesn't disappoint them. After every imaginable fireworks display, for a climax he has a mountain shooting forth colored flames, out of which emerges a dragon who flies three times over the head of the crowd before it finally explodes.

Bilbo, however, who had been on the quest for dragon treasure under Gandalf's leadership, knows that Gandalf is considerably more powerful than he lets on. They have become close friends over the years. And his nephew Frodo has also come to know and love Gandalf, and to see beneath the figure he shows to the crowd, to the greater man within.

> *Those who possess real wisdom often choose to conceal it. The wise man no longer has any need to prove himself wise. Those who need what they have to offer recognize the greater man within, while those who don't can deal with them at a level with which they feel comfortable.*

Bilbo wants one more adventure before he dies, and has decided to visit his elven friends in Rivendell, perhaps never to return. After Bilbo pulls his disappearing act at the climax of his birthday party, he returns to his house and prepares to leave. Gandalf comes in just as Bilbo is ready to go out the door with the Ring hidden in his pocket. When Gandalf first suggests, then insists, that he leave the Ring behind, Bilbo loses his temper and cries that the Ring is his to do with as he pleases. When he calls it "my precious,"[58] Gandalf says that it's been called that name before. And so it has, first by Isildur, who took it from Sauron's finger, then by Gollum. When Bilbo tries to leave with the Ring, Gandalf suddenly gives us a glimpse of who he really is; suddenly "his shadow filled the little room."[59] Bilbo backs away and says in bewilderment that he can't trust his mind. At that, Gandalf's menace drops away and he gently tells Bilbo that if he can't trust his own judgement, he should trust

Gandalf's, and give the Ring to Frodo. Finally Bilbo does leave the Ring behind, and goes on his way with a lighter heart.

> *This is the first instance where we see something of the greater Gandalf, when he seems to become physically larger. Tolkien will use that image many times in the book, not only for Gandalf, but for Aragorn and Frodo as well. It's difficult for someone to find a category in which they can "see" someone greater than themselves, so often they have to put them into convenient "containers" such as "bigger" or "stronger." But that simply means that the person cannot be contained within normal definitions.*

When Frodo arrives, Gandalf explains that Bilbo has gone, leaving him everything, including the Ring. "But keep it secret and keep it safe!"[60] Gandalf then takes his leave of Frodo, warning him that it may be a while before he returns. And when he does come back, he'll do so quietly, as rumors have spread in the Shire that he is responsible for Bilbo's unhobbitlike disappearance. As he leaves, "Frodo thought the old wizard looked unusually bent, almost as if he was carrying a great weight."[61]

> *With great wisdom comes great responsibility. As we grow in consciousness, we might think that life becomes easier, but it doesn't. Life demands ever more of us, constantly raising the stakes, asking us to see more deeply, to be more than we are.*

GANDALF TELLS FRODO THE STORY OF THE RING

Over the years that follow, there are increasingly longer periods of time between Gandalf's visits. Finally, after a nine-year absence, Frodo has come to wonder if he will ever see Gandalf again. Just at this point, Gandalf returns and tells Frodo the history of the Ring. Then he takes the Ring from Frodo and throws it into the fire. When characters appear in an ancient elven writing unknown to Frodo (who has himself learned a great deal of elven lore from Bilbo), Gandalf reads them for him. Though in elven characters, the language is of the dark land of Mordor. Translated into the common tongue of Middle-Earth, it says: "One Ring to rule them all, One Ring to find them, One Ring to bring them all and in the Darkness bind them."[62]

> *Everything that exists in the world has evolved over immense periods of time in order to properly fit into that world. In all creatures with a sufficiently complex neurological structure, the world is mirrored within that inner structure in complex ways. Thus the inside and the outside have become inseparable. Mathematician and philosopher Blaise Pascal said it this way: "It [where "it" might be nature, the universe, God] is an infinite sphere, the center of which is everywhere, the circumference nowhere.'[63] Well, Tolkien is saying something similar when he talks of the Rings for each race and the One ring which rules over all. Each of the races--Elves, Dwarves, men--can be viewed as a unity, a circle, a ring, and each of those rings connects with all the others. And in Tolkien's story, there is one ring, one such container that is more powerful than any other, and hence must be destroyed. But, of course, all are still ultimately linked, since the world is a unity.*

Gandalf then briefly tells Frodo how he's come to know about the Ring, and how Bilbo acquired it from Gollum, who is still at large in the world hunting for it. And that, worst of all, Sauron has learned from Gollum that the Ring still exists and that it may be in the Shire. When Frodo hears this, he says that it's a pity that Bilbo didn't kill Gollum. Gandalf answers "Pity? It was Pity that stayed his hand. Pity, and Mercy not to strike without need."[64] When Frodo isn't convinced and says that Gollum "deserves death," Gandalf tries to teach Frodo about life and death: that life isn't necessarily fair, that some good men die, while bad men live on. But that it is not within our power to play god and mete out death to anyone. "For even the wise cannot see all ends."[65]

Gandalf is certain that Gollum will play a necessary part in the events to come. He doesn't know whether his role will be for good or evil, but pity toward another creature is never wrong. Gandalf is right, of course, for without Gollum, the Ring would never have been destroyed. But for now, we simply see the depths of Gandalf's compassion, as it can extend even to a creature like Gollum. As we will see later in discussing Frodo's path, as Frodo's own wisdom and compassion grow, he comes to realize just how right Gandalf was.

With wisdom comes compassion. That is an invariable truth no matter what path one is on. Wisdom is quite different from mere knowledge or power. One can gain great knowledge, great power, and yet care little about others. But as wisdom grows, so does compassion.

After hearing that Sauron has his underlings searching for the Ring, Frodo agrees to take the Ring and leave the Shire. Gandalf is overcome with admiration for his bravery. Here is this little Hobbit, who has lived a life of comfort and ease, never wondering where his next meal, or even next pipe of tobacco, will come from. Yet, presented with a situation that would daunt the mightiest of warriors, Frodo is immediately willing to leave his comfortable life, with no idea of where he must go or what he must do. He knows only that the Ring must not fall into the hands of Sauron and that it is his task to carry it. We already see a glimpse of what greatness lies in Frodo, a greatness that will grow over the course of the quest.

In Frodo we see the one person who might someday be even greater than Gandalf.

GANDALF'S SEARCH FOR INFORMATION ABOUT THE ONE RING

We now need to break from the order in the books and tell Gandalf's story, as he presents it later at the Council of Elrond. The story begins nearly three thousand years earlier, at the end of the Second Age, after the defeat of Sauron and the loss of the Ring. At a great council held then, Saruman claimed that the One Ring had fallen into the river, where it was swept into the Sea to be lost forever. Gandalf tells the Council that he was at fault in so readily accepting Saruman's words, but Saruman was the leader of the Order of Wizards and, therefore, someone Gandalf trusted.

Wisdom only comes from searching within, but this is such a lonely process that inevitably we look outside us for direction. Often life is kind and does present us with guides along the way. But all too often guides can be false. Ultimately we can only trust our own inner sense of right and wrong.

That was why, when he later learned that Bilbo had taken a magical ring from Gollum, Gandalf was by no means sure that it was the One, and so let time pass, time which he could have used to find a way to dispose of the Ring forever. But when years later, he discovers spies of many kinds hunting for the Ring, he and Aragorn begin to hunt for Gollum—with no luck. Only then does Gandalf remember Saruman's description of the various rings. Saruman had said that the One Ring was plain, as if it were nothing special, except that it had marks on it that revealed its true identity.

We expect great things to look magnificent. It's hard to appreciate that something great can look ordinary. But just as Gandalf appears to most as a tired old man who can do a few simple parlor tricks, the One Ring appears to be much less than it really is.

So Gandalf goes to Gondor and, with Lord Denethor's grudging consent, hunts through the library of books and scrolls until he finally finds Isildur's description of the ring. It contains a copy of the script on the Ring, as well as the fact that the words had, over time, gradually faded. They could now only be read if the Ring was cast into a fire. Gandalf was eventually to read these dire words on the Ring in Frodo's possession, and know at last that it was the One Ring, the Ring that could give Sauron domination once more over everyone.

The words that reveal the "one" are always hidden and can only be read by someone who already possesses wisdom.

GANDALF'S IMPRISONMENT AND ESCAPE

Continuing his tale, Gandalf explains that, after leaving Frodo, he encountered a lesser wizard, but a brave and true one: Radagast the Brown. Radagast has been searching for Gandalf to bring him frightening news: the nine Nazgûl are once more out in the world, disguised as black riders. They are searching for something unknown, and asking for news about the Shire. Radagast says that Saruman the

White wants Gandalf to come to Isengard to confer with him. Just before they part, Gandalf asks Radagast to tell the birds and beasts to bring him any news they may have of these happenings. This afterthought will turn out to be providential for Gandalf.

In Greek mythology heroes were almost invariably flawed in some way. The most famous example is Achilles' Heel. When he was born, his mother Thetis held him by one heel and dipped him into the river Styx (i.e., death) in order to protect him. But this left that heel mortal, unprotected, and ultimately he was killed when Paris shot him with an arrow in his heel. The fatal flaw of Saruman and Sauron is their arrogance and contempt for so-called lesser beings. Saruman views Radagast as weak and ineffectual, yet he is really brave and true. Thus though Saruman tricks him into sending Gandalf to be captured, Radagast is also the source of Gandalf's rescue.

Gandalf comes to Saruman's stronghold of Orthanc in Isengard. From the start, we see a marked contrast between Saruman and Gandalf: while Gandalf may not suffer fools gladly, he is also kind to even the most foolish. Saruman is simply arrogant and rude, even to a fellow wizard. When Gandalf addresses him as Saruman the White, Saruman grows angry and says "I am Saruman, the Wise, Saruman Ring-maker, Saruman of many Colours!" When Gandalf says simply "I liked white better,"[66] Saruman softens his tone. He uses all his wiles to try and persuade Gandalf that it is impossible to resist Sauron, and that by joining with him, they may help create a grand new order. Gandalf sees through his sophistry and answers: "Well, the choices are, it seems, to submit to Sauron, or to yourself. I will take neither. Have you others to offer?"[67]

Though Saruman was considered the greater wizard, we already see that Gandalf has passed him up in true wisdom. It is telling that Saruman is no longer satisfied with being Saruman the White. He can't be Saruman the Black, since Sauron rules that kingdom, so he chooses the rainbow. There is an old saying that we can be anything we want to be in life, we just can't be everything. In order to grow, inevitably we have to make choices. And choosing one thing means that we leave another behind. So growth is always bitter-sweet. But those who, like Saruman, are vain and selfish, want everything.

That is too much for Saruman, who has his men take Gandalf to the top of Orthanc, from which there is seemingly no escape. Gandalf stays imprisoned there for some time, forced to watch helplessly as Saruman prepares his forces for the war to come. But eventually, the greatest of the Great eagles, Gwahir the Windlord, flies to Gandalf to bring him news, as Radagast had asked him to do. At Gandalf's request, Gwaihir flies him from Orthanc to Rohan.

Gandalf's rescue comes from two sources: from Radagast the Brown, who is connected with the earth and all its creatures; and from Gwaihir the Great Eagle, who rules the sky, the world of spirit. It is because Gandalf contains both earth and spirit within himself that no one can hold him prisoner for long.

GANDALF'S SEARCH FOR FRODO

In Rohan, Gandalf once more receives an unfriendly welcome. When King Théoden tells him to take a horse and leave, Gandalf chooses the finest horse in the kingdom, the finest horse in Middle Earth: Shadowfax.

Greatness recognizes greatness. Another seeming bromide that is as true today as it ever was.

Now able to move at great speed, Gandalf searches for Frodo, first finding news of him at the Prancing Pony from the innkeeper, Butterburr. He then gallops on to Weathertop, which he reaches before Frodo, Strider and their companions. The Riders are already there waiting for the Hobbits, but are afraid to confront Gandalf during the day. When night comes, however, they attack him in force, and he has a difficult time surviving the night, with odds of nine to one against him.

At this point, as great as Gandalf is, he is not yet capable of defeating all nine of the Nazgûl alone. This is a sign that Gandalf still has some growth to come.

When morning arrives, he flees toward the north, hoping to lead the Black Riders away from Frodo. He is successful in leading away four of the nine, so that only five attack Frodo's company. Otherwise, even with Strider's help, the Black Riders might well have prevailed and the story would have come to a sad end before it had hardly begun. Meanwhile, Gandalf sends Shadowfax away and arrives in Rivendell only three days before Frodo.

WHAT TO DO WITH THE RING?

With his story told and everyone now fully aware of the danger that the Ring presents, various suggestions are made by the company. When Elrond suggests that the Ring should be given to Bombadil for safe-keeping, since it has no power over him, Gandalf explains that Bombadil would probably also lose interest in it and eventually throw it away. He is simply not interested in things outside his own world. When the elven Lord Glorfindel suggests the Ring be cast into the deepest part of the sea, Gandalf reminds the company that the Ring is always seeking its master Sauron, and that while this might provide a brief solution to the problem, the council must take the long view, and find a way to solve the problem forever.

Wisdom invariably looks at the big picture.

When his listeners begin to despair, Gandalf counsels that: "Despair is only for those who see the end beyond all doubt. We do not."[68] Eventually they all agree reluctantly that the Ring must be destroyed once and for all, and since the only way to do that is to throw it into the fire where it was created, it must be taken to Mount Doom in the Heart of Mordor. When Frodo bravely agrees to carry the Ring, the fellowship forms, with Gandalf as its leader, and Strider, now revealed as Aragorn, at his side.

When the fellowship forms, it is the wisest who lead. Within the many parts of our own personalities, while each have their role to play, we need to look to the wise old man within to lead us.

GANDALF LEADS THE COMPANY, THEN THE COMPANY LOSES ITS LEADER

Their first great challenge is on Caradhras the Cruel, where the company is forced to try to make a fire or die. When, with the wind and the wet wood, neither man nor Elf nor Dwarf can light a fire, Gandalf is forced to use his staff and magic words. He knows that he might as well have written his name in large letters for Saruman's and Sauron's spies. They survive the night, but are eventually defeated by Caradhras. Gandalf says that they must now take a worse road, through the Mines of Moria.

> *There are forces of nature that are beyond us. When we encounter such primal challenges in our life, we must always be wise enough to accept defeat. Gandalf has tried to go over Caradhras, to get up above the problem, but he finds that instead he has to go below, into the Mines of Moria, to dig into his own depths. Ultimately that is where the deepest fear lies, even for one as wise as Gandalf.*

During the night, the company is attacked by wolves, "Hounds of Sauron," as Gandalf calls them. Legolas kills their leader when it attacks Gandalf, but the wolves regroup, then attack in force. Aragorn and Boromir, Gimli and Legolas, each defends bravely, but the company would not have survived without Gandalf. He becomes suddenly larger than life, then takes a burning branch and approaches the wolves. Chanting a magic phrase, he tosses the branch into the air, and suddenly a magical fire crowns all the treetops. With their battle ground now lit like it was day, the rest of the company rushes against the wolves, and sends them fleeing for their lives. As Sam tells Pippin of Gandalf's feat, "That was an eye-opener, and no mistake! Nearly singed the hair off my head!"[69] In the morning, however, there are no wolf bodies to be found. They were truly "Hounds of Sauron."

> *We increasingly see Gandalf having to exert his power in the world, a sign that the challenges are growing.*

In the previous chapter, we discussed the adventures of Gandalf and his friends in the Mines of Moria, but left his encounter with the Balrog for this chapter, since it is a turning point in Gandalf's long life. The

Balrog is an ancient and evil creature, going back to the First Age of Middle Earth. It remained hidden at the core of the mithril vein in Khazad-dûm until accidentally released when Dwarves mined the mithril. Once released, it killed many of the Dwarves, including two of their kings, before they fled Khazad-dûm. When Sauron rose again in the Third Age, he sent Orcs and trolls to dwell there, where they were ruled by the Balrog entirely through their fear of it. In this Third Age, only Sauron is a more powerful force of evil.

As a representation of an evil that goes back almost before time, the Balrog is clearly impossible for anyone to truly describe. He would best be left to our imaginations, as is Sauron, who we only encounter indirectly throughout the books. But since there needs to be a physical confrontation with Gandalf, Tolkien does the best he can, and presents a truly awful creature. But clearly, what he would like us to call up within is something greater than anything he can show us, something hidden in our darkest fears.

When the Balrog comes, Gandalf leads the others safely across the bridge out into the outer world, then remains behind on the bridge and turns to fight. The Balrog advances, but Gandalf holds forth his sword Glamdring and cries: "You cannot pass."[70] Each time the Balrog tries to advance, Gandalf repeats this cry. Their swords clash and that of the Balrog melts, but he moves forward again, whip in hand. Gandalf strikes the bridge with his staff. The staff breaks, a flame shoots up, and the bridge cracks at the Balrog's feet. As he falls into the abyss beneath, his whip cracks one final time and catches Gandalf around his knees, dragging him down with the Balrog. As Gandalf falls, he cries to the others "Fly, you fools!"[71] That is the last that they will see of him until he reappears later, transformed. Meanwhile, the rest of the fellowship mourns Gandalf and proceeds on their way, filled with grief at the loss of their leader.

This is a pivotal event in the trilogy. To this point, Gandalf has been the leader, the one everyone turns to not only for his wisdom, but also, when all else has failed, for his power. And now he is gone. At some time in our life, each of us reaches a place where everything and everyone we have looked to for support fail us and we have to depend on our own resources. That's a frightening time, but a necessary step in growth.

GANDALF THE WHITE

Only much later, after the rest of the company has many adventures that we've discussed in the previous two chapters, does Gandalf reappear. After entering the forest of Fangorn, Legolas, Gimli and Aragorn see an old man, dressed in dirty grey rags, moving slowly, leaning on his staff as he goes. Thinking it is Saruman, Gimli tells Legolas to shoot him with his bow and arrow, but when Legolas tries to do so, the bow and arrow drop from his hand, though he is allowed to pick them up again.

When Aragorn asks for his name, the old man asks if they haven't already guessed it. He then tries to get them to tell him their tale, but when they stand silent, he tells them, rather obliquely, that Merry and Pippin are safe with Treebeard. As he sits down, his rags part and they see that beneath his rags, he is clad entirely in white. They are now convinced that he is Saruman. But when they try to attack him, he simply lifts his staff and Gimli's axe falls to the ground, Aragorn's sword freezes in his grasp, and Legolas' arrow shoots high into the air and vanishes in flames.

At that, they realize who it is, and cry out "Gandalf." When Gandalf hears that name, he has to say it over to himself, as if trying to remember who Gandalf was. When Gimli laughs and remarks that he is all in white now, Gandalf replies "Yes, I am white now. Indeed I am Saruman, one might almost say. Saruman as he should have been."[72]

And so he is "Saruman as he should have been." Saruman the White, leader of his order, failed in his appointed task, and so Gandalf has been transformed into the wise man Saruman should have been. When something is lacking, something else fills the void.

When Aragorn remarks that Gandalf still talks in riddles, Gandalf corrects him and says that he was merely talking to himself: "A habit of the old: they choose the wisest person present to speak to; the long explanations needed by the young are wearying."[73] And then he laughs warmly.

We remarked earlier that with wisdom also comes compassion. Interestingly, so does humor. Wise people laugh a lot, though often times no one else understands why.

At their prodding, Gandalf tells as much as he wishes to share of his ordeal with the Balrog. For a long time, the two fall together. Gandalf is burned by the Balrog's fire until they fall into deep, dark water, so cold it "almost froze my heart,"[74] but thankfully it also quenches the Balrog's fire. When finally they reach the stone foundations at the core of the earth, they once more fight. They fight until the Balrog flees into the tunnels of the earth, tunnels far more ancient than those made by the Dwarves, tunnels made by vile creatures older even than Sauron. In those dark regions, Gandalf himself despairs and can do no more than to follow the Balrog, hoping he would find a way out of these depths.

The Balrog is a being of pure fire. In all spiritual traditions, fire is a transformative element. Gandalf is forced to struggle with the Balrog in order to be transformed. He must go down to his deepest depths and struggle with the darkness he finds there. There is no path to wisdom that does not include that inner journey. Perhaps the most famous expression of this inner journey is St. John of the Cross' "Dark night of the soul," but it has found expression in the mystical literatures of all cultures. In Jungian psychology, this is called the confrontation with the Shadow. In our deep inner self, we find not only all that is evil and, like the Balrog, must be rejected, but we also find all that has never seen the light and needs to be mined. Tolkien is wise enough to place this action off-stage, so that it is left to the reader's imagination. But the entire description, brief as it is, can be interpreted symbolically. Each part has some clue for us to survive our own inner battle.

The two come up into Dwarf tunnels, those of the ancient Dwarf city of Khazad-dûm, and then to the Endless Stair, which stretches over thousands of steps from the dungeons to the pinnacle: Durin's Tower. There they fight again, until Gandalf throws the Balrog down to be crushed against the sides of the mountain. Then Gandalf falls into unconsciousness, and in that state, walks over roads that know neither thought nor time.

From the depths, one has to come to the peaks in trying to resolve this inner issue. And eventually, one has to simply give up one's former state of conscious being, and walk without identity over timeless roads. This can take a very long time, or take place instantly, as in Zen tales of transformation.

Eventually he emerges naked, reborn, to complete his task on this earth. He lies on a mountain top until once more his friend, the great Eagle Gwaihir the Windlord finds him and takes him to Galadriel in Lothlórien.

When, after passing through our individual dark night of the soul, we reemerge, we are necessarily naked; that is, we no longer have our old persona, the face we present to the world. But note that, while transformed from Gandalf the Grey into Gandalf the White, he is still Gandalf. All too often, people on spiritual paths get confused about this and think that somehow they should be other than who they are. But we are each unique, and our possibilities are unique unto us. As poet William Wordsworth said: "the child is father of the man." At the end of each of our journeys, we arrive to find the child looking at us.

With his transformation complete, it is time once more for action. Gandalf provides encouragement for his companions. Though they are fighting both Sauron and Saruman, the pair make uneasy allies, each seeking the Ring for their own profit, each concealing much from the other. And, ironically, all their efforts to find the Ring have only driven Merry and Pippin into Fangorn, which in turn has roused Treebeard and the Ents against Saruman. Gimli asks Gandalf if Treebeard is dangerous, and Gandalf says that he certainly is. But so is Gandalf himself, and so too are Aragorn and Legolas and Gimli dangerous. The Ents are only dangerous to those who threaten their existence and now that they know that Saruman is killing trees, they are very dangerous indeed—for Saruman. Though the transformed Gandalf is now a much more powerful person than Gandalf the Grey, he reminds them while he may be Gandalf the White, "Black is mightier still."[75]

Even transformed, Gandalf knows his limitations. It is always wise when we deal with darkness, including the darkness within each of us, to realize its power and our own limitations.

Now that Merry and Pippin are safe with Treebeard, Gandalf tells them that it is time for their search to end. Now is the time to find allies for the war to come, and so they must go with him to Rohan to see King Théoden. Aragorn says that while Sauron might have the nine Black Riders, they have the White Rider, who is greater than all. This is a telling statement by Aragorn: while Gandalf the Grey had to summon all his resources merely to survive against the nine, now Aragorn is confident that Gandalf the White is more powerful than all nine combined.

GANDALF GIVES KING THÉODEN NEW LIFE

When Gandalf and his friends arrive at Rohan, King Théoden's men are far from welcoming, saying that Wormtongue, speaking for the king, has ordered that no strangers be admitted to Rohan. Though the company is finally admitted, they are forced to leave their weapons behind. When Aragorn bridles at this, Gandalf tells him that while Théoden's demand might be unnecessary, there is no point in refusing it: "A king will have his way in his own hall, be it folly or wisdom."[76] Gandalf then gives up his own sword as a sign to his companions to follow. When Gandalf is asked to also give up his staff, he slyly argues that he's old and needs his staff to lean on. If he can't do so, he'll have to stay outside and the king will have to come to him. Though the guard, Hama, is not fooled by Gandalf's deception, he believes in his good faith and allows Gandalf to bear his staff.

Wisdom knows when to bow to established power, but also knows not to relinquish all its own power. In large part, as one grows in wisdom, one has to learn how to deal with the power that accompanies wisdom. It can neither be denied nor abused. If one tries to refuse the power as something inherently evil, it turns on its possessor. Gandalf knows exactly how to walk the fine line between those extremes.

Once in the king's hall, they find Théoden stooped with age, barely able to rise, with the help of a staff, to meet them. He is sharp with Gandalf, who he says comes only with bad tidings. His evil counselor Wormtongue steps in to insidiously expand on this theme, calling Gandalf "Master Stormcrow"[77] Gandalf doesn't rise to the bait, but points out that there are two types who bear bad tidings: those who themselves are evil, and those who come to help in a bad time. Wormtongue, overstepping his bounds, says that there is a third type: the vultures who feed on the sorrow of others.

It is fascinating that Gandalf, so famously short-tempered with even those he loves like Merry and Pippin, remains patiently restrained in the face of insults from Wormtongue. Wisdom knows when to bide its time.

Still Gandalf holds his temper in check, merely reminding Théoden that his hall was once famed for its courtesy, and that it has seldom had such visitors as he brings with him. When Wormtongue interjects that they are in league with the "Sorceress of the Golden Wood,"[78] Gimli is only held back from striking him by Gandalf. But, Gandalf, too, has finally had enough. He tosses aside his cloak, stands to his full height, and holds forth his staff. When Wormtongue begins once more to spread his venom, Gandalf merely gestures with the staff and Wormtongue falls on his belly like the snake he is.

When Gandalf does choose to act, his power is immense. Again a portrait of wisdom.

But it's not Wormtongue that Gandalf is concerned with, but Théoden. He gently invites the king to come out of his dark hall into the sunlight. When Théoden does and looks around him, he sees that it's not really as dark as he Wormtongue had led him to believe. When Gandalf then tells him to cast aside his staff, it falls from his hand and he slowly stands upright again. "Dark have been my dreams of late, but I feel as one reawakened."[79]

Gandalf then asks him to send for his beloved nephew Éomer, who he has imprisoned at Wormtongue's instigation. His only crime was that he disagreed with the king and warned that the kingdom must prepare for war. Gandalf tells Théoden that this is exactly what he must do. Having brought him into the light and made him stand upright without his staff, Gandalf now gives the king a third gift: he tells him "Your fingers would remember their old strength better if they grasped a sword-hilt."[80]

The king can't remember where Wormtongue has put it, but Éomer steps forth, kneels and lays his own sword at the feet of the king. When Théoden grasps the sword, the last part of his rebirth takes place and he raises it into the air, with a war cry that makes his men all lay their swords at his feet and say simply "Command us!"[81] From this point on, Théoden is once more the wise, brave, and generous king Gandalf had previously known and loved.

We see how carefully Gandalf has restored the king to his former power. The reawakening has been gradual, so that the king can adjust to each step. This is how wisdom teaches.

But there is still one final matter to deal with: Wormtongue. He is brought forth and revealed to be a spy of Saruman. Even knowing this, Théoden is merciful, telling Wormtongue that he can either ride to war with his king or leave the kingdom, never to return. Wormtongue slinks away, back to his true Lord and Master, Saruman. Théoden and his men, together with Aragorn, Legolas, and Gimli ride on to Helm's Deep, while Gandalf, the White Rider, rides off alone on Shadowfax to gather other troops to aid in the battle.

SARUMAN MEETS THE TRANSFORMED GANDALF

When Gandalf and his companions, along with King Théoden and his men, arrive at Isengard, they find that Treebeard has taken full control and has Saruman isolated in his tower, Orthanc, accompanied by his venomous servant Wormtongue. Despite knowing that it is probably a useless gesture, Gandalf tries to talk fairly with Saruman one more time, giving him an opportunity to cast off his evil and return to the greatness that once was his. He warns his companions to be careful, as even Saruman's tongue can be a weapon to be feared.

As we've said, with wisdom invariably comes compassion. That Gandalf's compassion extends even to Saruman is remarkable.

Gandalf beats at the door of the tower with his staff, calling for Saruman to come out and show himself. And when he does, he begins to talk, and as Gandalf warned, his voice alone is enough to enchant his listeners. Once Saruman the White, he had become Saruman of Many Colors and the onlookers find it difficult to pin down exactly what they see, since their view is constantly changing. He turns his attention first to Théoden, and tries to persuade him that they are friends and natural allies. When the listeners begin to fall under his spell, Gimli sees through his lies and growls that "The words of this wizard stand on their heads."[82]

Because Gimli is rooted in the earth, he is less prone to fall under Saruman's spell. When we need to judge the difference between wisdom and sophistry, it is wise to turn to the Gimli within.

Saruman is briefly disconcerted at this interruption, but quickly turns again to his attempt to corrupt Théoden. When Théoden remains silent, his nephew Éomer fears that he is under Saruman's spell and pleads with him. Saruman once more reacts first with anger, then with honeyed tongue, finally asking "Théoden King: shall we have peace and friendship, you and I? It is ours to command."[83]

When Théoden answers "We will have peace," everyone fears that he has fallen under Saruman's spell. But Théoden reveals his returned greatness when he continues "Yes, we will have peace, when you and all your works have perished."[84]

A king returned to power cannot be deceived by such as Saruman. He can hear the difference between real wisdom from Gandalf, and sophistry from Saruman.

His words shake the cobwebs off of everyone's minds and they are no longer under Saruman's spell. Saruman is too angry to contain himself any longer. He turns to bitter insults instead of sweet compliments, then, exhausting that outlet, turns finally to Gandalf, appealing to him as a fellow wizard. Saruman uses every charm at his disposal at this point, so that everyone listening hears "the gentle remonstrance of a kindly king with an erring but much-loved minister."[85] They feel left out in the cold, isolate from this pair of equals who are clearly of a higher stripe than they could ever aspire to be. They are sure that Gandalf will, of course, once more align himself with this great man. Even Théoden wonders if perhaps Gandalf might betray them all. But all doubts fade when Gandalf merely laughs at Saruman. "Saruman, you missed your path in life. You should have been the king's jester."[86]

If Saruman cannot fool Gimli or Théoden, how can he possibly fool Gandalf?

Then Gandalf kindly asks Saruman for one last time if he might not trust him, and come down from his tower, and go on his way. Since Saruman would never show such kindness to a defeated enemy, he distrusts Gandalf, no matter how much Gandalf reassures him that he will be allowed to leave in freedom. When Saruman turns haughtily to return inside his tower, Gandalf's friendly tone dies away and he calls him back with a voice that must be obeyed. Saruman returns to the parapet, as if he is a puppet under Gandalf's control. Gandalf tells him sternly that he is no longer Gandalf the Grey, but now Gandalf the White, and he has taken Saruman's place as the chief of all wizards. With a gesture of his hand, he commands Saruman's magical staff to break apart, and, with that symbolic act, forever casts Saruman out of the Council of Wizards.

Compassion extends only so far. There will always be those who misunderstand kindness as weakness; with such people, one has to be firm.

Even after all this, Gandalf is merciful. When Pippin asks him what he will do to Saruman if somehow they triumph over Sauron, Gandalf says he will do nothing. Gandalf is not interested in mastery.

While wisdom inherently creates power, and one has to accept that power, there is no desire for power for its own sake. Again Gandalf is a fine example of how wisdom uses but doesn't abuse its power.

GANDALF, DENETHOR AND THE SIEGE OF GONDOR

His next stop is Gondor. While Gandalf was able to restore King Théoden to his greatness, Lord Denethor, Steward of Gondor, is beyond Gandalf's help. When Gandalf comes to Denethor, warning him of the dangers at hand, Denethor berates Gandalf for not giving him the Ring. Like Boromir, he can think no further than his own land of Gondor, and the possibility that the Ring could over-master him is beyond his imagination. Once a great man, a king in all but name, he was tempted by his arrogance to look into a Palantir and try his wits against Sauron. Though strong enough that he never becomes a total servant of Sauron like the Black Riders, Sauron nevertheless twists his values until he no longer knows right from wrong.

Here we see a counter-example to Gandalf. Denethor assumes the mantle of wisdom without going through the inner battle necessary to possess it. Because he is not truly wise, he desires power that exceeds his capabilities.

He loved his brave but arrogant and impetuous elder son Boromir too much, and his wise younger son Faramir too little, dismissing the latter as a "wizard's pupil."[87] With Boromir dead and Denethor isolated in his chamber, Gondor desperately needs Faramir—who is loved and respected by all save his father—at home as a visible leader for his people. But Denethor sees in Faramir only a reminder of his dead son, Boromir. To keep Faramir from his sight, Denethor constantly sends him away from the city on increasingly dangerous missions. As Faramir leaves on his last mission, the defense of the outpost at Osgliath, he tells his father "Then farewell! But if I should return, think better of me!" Even in this moment, Denethor does not bend and answers "That depends on the manner of your return."[88] It is left to Gandalf to tell Faramir that, despite his words, his father loves him, and that he should not throw his life away, for he is needed at home.

Because Denethor puts too much value on the wrong qualities, he fails to see potential greatness when it is right before him in his son Faramir.

Because of Denethor's foolish actions, when the enemy lays siege to Gondor, and Faramir is badly needed at home, he instead lies wounded at Osgliath, to be brought home in a coma. As the battle rages, Faramir lies unconscious and feverish, fighting for his life. And so Gandalf the wizard is forced to take command of the forces of Gondor. Gandalf's mere presence cheers the forces of Gondor, but they are vastly outnumbered. When the great Gate of Gondor falls, Gandalf stands alone to face the leader of the enemy—the Lord of the Nazgûl. Happily, at that moment, Théoden arrives with the forces of Rohan.

With the battle raging back and forth, and Gandalf racing from one defensive position to another, once more Denethor's foolish pride threatens Gondor's security; he finally realizes his love for Faramir, but it is a love so mixed with self-love that he feels he is entitled to control Faramir's life and death. As a final act of pride, he tries to immolate both Faramir and himself.

Denethor's final foolishness nearly proves fatal to Faramir. What is so sad here is that there is greatness in Denethor, but power abused, knowledge abused, destroys him.

Except for Pippin's quick actions Denethor would have been successful. Nevertheless, in order to save Faramir, Gandalf is forced to leave the battle at just the point when he is most needed. Denethor stands as a prime example of just what a king, or in his case, an aspirant to be a king, should not be. We will see just the opposite in the next chapter, when we discuss Aragorn and the Path of the King. As we will see, it is Aragorn's arrival that saves Gondor. But again this is Gandalf's tale we are telling, so we move forward in time.

THE BLACK GATE

After defeating the enemy at Gondor, Aragorn and Gandalf gather their army together and make their way toward Mordor. Aragorn does his best to spread out his forces so that they look as impressive as possible. But with many of their forces already dead, and a large number of those remaining necessarily left to defend Gondor and Rohan, or take back outposts still held by the enemy, there are less than six thousand troops left when they arrive at the Black Gate: the entrance to Mordor. Once his forces are in place, Aragorn has the heralds blow their trumpets and call for Sauron to come forth and face justice. But all know that they are merely whistling in the dark.

Sauron, ever the master of fear, has his forces reply with a cacophony of drums and horns that shake the ground and deafen the forces of the West. A rider then emerges from the center of the Gate, dressed all in black, riding a black steed. He is not one of the Nazgûl, but a still living man, the Lieutenant of the Tower. He announces himself as "the Mouth of Sauron,"[89] and so he is; little more than an instrument to carry Sauron's message. And an insulting message it is. He first mocks Aragorn and his army, then turns to Gandalf with his real message. Guards bring forth a bundle containing Sam's sword, an elven cloak and brooch, and Frodo's armor of mithril-mail, wrapped in his clothes. On seeing these, everyone feels as if their last hope has been vanished, along with Frodo and Sam. They have no idea that, in fact, Frodo and Sam are still alive within Mordor itself, struggling toward Mount Doom.

Sauron's mouthpiece presents Gandalf with humiliating terms in exchange for the lives of the Hobbits, which of course, are not theirs to give. But lies are Sauron's stock-in-trade. Knowing how outnumbered they are, and disheartened by what they've seen, everyone expects Gandalf to accept Sauron's terms. But instead he throws open his cloak and lets the radiance of Gandalf the White shine forth. He advances on Sauron's emissary, takes Sam's and Frodo's belongings, then waves Sauron's mouthpiece away, like he's dealing with a rat that should slink back into its hole.

> *There comes a time on the path of wisdom when one must simply stand up and declare what is right and what is wrong, despite overwhelming odds. It is easy to stand for the right when times are easy. It is when things are at their worst that we must find that courage.*

At Gandalf's refusal, once more horns sound from beyond the Black Gate, then all the doors open at once and a huge army bursts forth. At the same time armies of Orcs stream down from the hills to cut off

Aragorn's forces from the rear. In total, the forces of the West are outnumbered more than ten to one. Finally, as if to settle the issue once and for all, out fly the Nazgûl on their winged steeds.

Aragorn and his forces battle with the bravery of those who, because they know they are going to die, want to make their death memorable. At that point, Gandalf stands on a hilltop and cries that "The Eagles are coming!"[90] And so they are, led by Gandalf's great friend, Gwaihir the Windlord. As the eagles swoop down, the Nazgûl flee. And, precisely at that moment, Frodo achieves his mission and the One Ring is destroyed in Mount Doom (of which we will say more in the chapter on Gollum). With the destruction of the Ring, so dies Sauron's power. Tolkien uses the image of ants wandering aimlessly after their queen has died, and it is an apt one, for Sauron's mighty army loses all coherence and flees in every direction, with Aragorn and his men chasing them.

While Gandalf is the leader of the forces of the West, they are made up of strong individuals: Aragorn, Legolas, Gimli, Théoden, Éomer, and all the others. In contrast, the forces of Sauron have no individuality and fall apart when Sauron dies. Within our own personalities, though wisdom should lie at the center, there are many parts that can stand alone when needed. Each of us is a community.

But Gandalf has still another mission; to try and get to Frodo and Sam before the Nazgûl. He asks Gwaihir, along with several other great eagles to carry not only him, but Frodo and Sam… if they are in time. And, of course they do arrive on time, but again that is a story for later chapters.

THE END OF THE THIRD AGE

With this final act, Gandalf's story is essentially over. With the Third Age ending, the time for Elves and wizards has also come to an end. From this time on, men will rule their own destinies without their aid. Gandalf is wise enough to recognize this. To emphasize this, Tolkien has him point it out explicitly several times: to Treebeard, when he explains that the new age of men may outlast even the Ents; to Saruman, when he encounters him in rags; to Butterbur when they pass through his inn; to

Merry and Pippin, when he says that they no longer need his help in handling the problems they encounter on returning to the Shire.

And so Gandalf joins Elrond and Galadriel, and the Elf-friends Bilbo and Frodo, and sails away over the Sea to the immortal lands of the Elves.

Chapter Four
The Path of the King

Of all the major figures in *The Lord of the Rings*, Aragorn comes closest to presenting the classic Path of the hero. The hero is born to his destiny, yet has to first lower himself and serve others before he can gradually come to claim his crown. Often the story begins with the dotage or death of the old king, followed by some great task which only the greatest hero can perform. Finally, having accomplished this task, the hero is not only crowned as the new king, but also often marries the princess, who becomes his queen.

This story, in all its many variants, has appeared over and over across time because it reflects an inner journey: the growth that must occur inside each of us in order to find our essential identity. We all contain greatness within, but we must first lower ourselves and perform menial tasks which teach us values that we could never otherwise learn. Then we must face a series of increasingly difficult challenges. With each success, we gain confidence. With each failure, we learn our limitations. Finally we face some ultimate challenge, which at base is always the same: the need for the reconciliation of the opposition between the two sides of our identity: the transient, physical being we normally consider to be who we are, with the transcendent being within, who is everything we might be. Following this path and solving that final challenge is what transforms a hero into a king.

In Aragorn's case, that opposition is emphasized. Though he is the heir of the great kings of old, when put to the test of the Ring, his ancestor Isildur failed his test of character. Aragorn fears that he—who carries Isildur's blood inside him—may also fail. In following Aragorn's story, we learn what it takes to be a hero, what we need to do to become a king.

MEETING STRIDER AT THE PRANCING PONY

We first encounter Aragorn sitting in a dark corner at the Inn of the Prancing Pony in Bree, closely watching Frodo and his companions. He's described as a "strange-looking weather-beaten"[91] man, wearing good clothes that fit him well, but which show hard use. Hardly a portrait we associate with a king. When Frodo, going under the name of Underhill, asks the innkeeper, Butterbur, about this stranger who is eying him, he is told that he is a Ranger known as Strider. The Rangers are a group of tough wandering men who the villagers mistrust. The villagers don't realize that the Rangers are actually their protectors, the reason why the residents of Bree can live quiet lives in safe homes. Butterbur says that Strider keeps to himself and rarely talks, but when he does talk, he can tell some very interesting tales.

> *Though it's hard to believe, given how perfectly Strider evolves before our eyes into Aragorn and finally into king Elessar, when Tolkien first wrote this description of Strider, he did not know himself who this dark stranger was and what he would become. Tolkien was not even sure yet whether he was friend or foe. The unconscious produced this image for him, and in the unconscious Strider was already a king.*

When Frodo foolishly slips on the Ring and vanishes in the inn, Strider is the first person he sees when he reappears. He immediately bawls Frodo out for his foolishness, then says that he wants a word with him later in private. Frodo doesn't know what to make of Strider. When later the Hobbits return to their room, Strider is already sitting there, smoking a pipe and waiting for them. They are upset to find that he already knows both Frodo's true identity and, even more significantly, his errand. Strider warns them about the Black Riders and says that he wants to accompany them on their journey.

Sam is suspicious of this hard-looking, dark man, and wants nothing to do with him, but Frodo is already seeing beneath the surface to the quality beneath. Still he remains unsure until Butterbur pops into the room; he's suddenly remembered a letter from Gandalf for Mr. Underhill that he had forgotten to send to the Shire. In the letter, Gandalf tells

Frodo that a friend named Strider can help them, but to make sure it's the real Strider, whose true name is Aragorn. Then he adds this poem:

All that is gold does not glitter,

Not all those who wander are lost;

The old that is strong does not wither,

Deep roots are not reached by the frost.

From the ashes a fire shall be woken,

A light from the shadows shall spring;

Renewed shall be blade that was broken,

The crownless again shall be king.[92]

The poem was written many years earlier by Bilbo when he first came to know Aragorn and his story. Every line is significant. "All that is gold does not glitter" turns the famous aphorism "all that glitters is not gold"[93] on its head in order to indicate that true greatness doesn't necessary show itself to the casual eye. "Not all those who wander are lost" is a reference to the Rangers, who wander near and far in order to protect the region from those who would do it harm. "The old that is strong does not wither, Deep roots are not reached by the frost" is more ambiguous and refers to the long blood line that connects Aragorn to the great kings of old. "From the ashes a fire shall be woken, A light from the shadows shall spring" describes his destiny. "Renewed shall be blade that was broken" tells of the sword he carries, the sword once used by his ancestor King Elendil, which broke when he fell at Sauron's feet. "The crownless again shall be king" explicitly describes Aragorn's state: believing his line cursed by Isildur's greed for the Ring, Aragorn has turned aside from his destiny to be king of all the lands, and instead elected to lead his men as simple Rangers. But this king without a crown will yet be king.

Even after hearing the letter, Sam still doubts him. When Sam asks how they know he's the real Strider, he laughs and tells them that they will just have to trust him. "If I was after the Ring, I could have it -

NOW!"[94] And at that, he suddenly grows taller and more menacing, much as Gandalf does several times in the book. Then, again like Gandalf, he returns to normal and smiles, assuring them that he is indeed Strider. Then for the first time in the book, we see intimations that he is the king-to-be when he adds with quiet dignity: "I am Aragorn son of Arathorn; and if by life or death I can save you, I will."[95] Then, to Frodo's surprise, he quotes from the poem in the letter, which Frodo has not yet read aloud to the others, and tells Frodo that the poem is about him. He draws forth his sword and shows that it is broken, as in the poem. "Not much use, is it, Sam?"[96] At that, they finally all accept him as their guide, though Sam is still suspicious.

As we saw with Gandalf, and will see again with Frodo, greatness cannot readily be recognized by most. In order to make itself manifest, it has to take some symbolic form we are all familiar with, such as size. The fact that Frodo sees so quickly beneath the veneer is simply an example of quality knowing quality.

The first thing Strider does is to move them from their room, since he knows the Black Riders will be coming. And, in fact, when the Hobbits wake in the morning and return to their room, they find it torn to pieces! Not only that, but their ponies are gone from the stable, as is every other horse in the inn. Though Frodo is despondent, Strider points out that they were hardly going to escape the Black Riders on their little ponies, and that they are probably better off going on foot and taking back ways not readily accessible to the Riders. His only worry is being able to carry enough food for their trip to Rivendell.

WEATHERTOP

In an effort to make it more difficult for the Black Riders to follow, Strider leads the company through marshy areas filled with flies and midges, much to the discomfort of the Hobbits. Each night, as the Hobbits sleep, Strider stands watch over them. Five days out they leave the marshes and can now see the Western Hills ahead of them. The tallest and most southerly of the hills is Weathertop, where they hoped to meet Gandalf, since he wasn't in Bree. Strider has mixed feelings about going there, as it is also likely to attract the Black Riders. But since he can't overlook any chance at meeting Gandalf, he decides to take a circuitous route in order to approach Weathertop from the North, rather than directly from the West.

Aragorn is familiar with the territory because he has long before left the well-traveled roads that most take and explored every part of the territory. No one can find who they are unless they leave the main roads and explore the areas overlooked by others.

Along the way, Strider shares ancient lore of the region with the Hobbits, making them wonder just who this strange man actually is. As they get closer to Weathertop, Strider becomes edgier, almost as irritable as Gandalf would be. Only he knows just how perilous their situation is. When Frodo jokes that's he's in danger of losing so much weight that he'll become a wraith, Strider blurts out "do not speak of such things!"[97] Later, when Pippin merely mentions Mordor, Strider cautions "do not speak that name so loudly."[98]

We see early that Strider has actual experience of evil, while the Hobbits have been able to live protected lives. Again there is no way to advance without coming to know evil and its consequences.

When they reach the base of Weathertop, they immediately begin to climb, since there is no longer any way to conceal themselves if the enemy is about. Partway up, they find a hollow where Sam and Pippin stay with the provisions. Another half-hour's hard climbing brings Strider to the top, to be followed a little later by an exhausted Merry and Frodo. Weathertop, like Stonehenge, is ringed by large stones, with a cairn of broken stones piled in the middle. Everything on the hilltop has been burned to the ground, seemingly recently, leaving only blackened stones. From their position, they have a birds-eye view for miles around on all sides happily, they see no movement anywhere around them.

Strider looks carefully for any sign that Gandalf might have left them. On top of the cairn he finds a single stone, which is both whiter and flatter than any of the others. It has some ambiguous scratches on it, which he thinks might be a glyph for G—Gandalf—followed by three vertical lines. He speculates that if this was a signal Gandalf left for them, it might mean that he was there on the 3rd of October, which was three days earlier. And, further, if Gandalf had to leave such a quickly inscribed, highly ambiguous message, he must have been in danger. Extrapolating from these small clues, Strider guesses that Gandalf might have fought on Weathertop, and the burnt condition was a reminder of what had occurred. Throughout the book, we have many such examples of Strider's incredible ability to interpret the meaning of small signs. For example, when much later, he, Legolas and Gimli examine the site where the riders of Rohan killed the band of Orcs, Strider is able to use the few signs available to correctly guess not only that at least one of Merry or Pippin escaped, but the circumstances that led to their escape.

> *This ability to read the essence of a situation from tiny clues is one that has to be developed by anyone who follows the path of individuation, which invariable leads us deep within ourselves into unexplored territory. It is easy to get lost in the unconscious, where symbols take the place of words and normal time and space have no meaning. We have to learn to read the symbols we find within if we are to keep advancing toward our destiny. Eventually we come to see that our outer lives are equally filled with symbolic meaning, so that we can both live life and observe it at the same time.*

With no Gandalf to guide them, they are now clearly on their own. Almost immediately they feel the presence of the Black Riders. When Merry and Frodo look again, now they see vague black shapes in the near distance. Aragorn, whose eyesight is almost uncanny (though even he can't match Legolas), can see the Black Riders clearly. The three hasten to join Sam and Pippin, who have found water, firewood, and footprints. Strider examines the signs there as well. Though he can't be sure, because much of the evidence has been trampled over by Sam and Pippin, he concludes that his fellow Rangers have left the firewood, but that there were other, more recent, heavily-booted tracks. It seems like a good time to leave, but Strider can think of no better place to hide before nightfall, so they settle down in the hollow for the night.

When Merry asks if the Black Riders can actually see them, Strider explains that while they can't see in the sense that we see, people and objects leave traces in their minds. And their horses can see, and they can sense the reactions of the horses. The Rider's keenest sense is that of smell: they smell—with disgust—the blood of anything living. But, above all, they are pulled by the Ring, as if there were a living connection between them and it. And so there is, for the Ring and Sauron are one, and the Black Riders are but appendages of Sauron.

Some critics have criticized Tolkien's story of a battle between good and evil as simplistic, but anyone who follows an inner path learns to discriminate between two versions of evil. Initially, since everything we encounter in the unconscious is just that—not conscious—all seems evil. But as we become more familiar with the inner territory, we learn to discriminate. We find that all the possibilities for our growth are hidden within the darkness. In the struggle between our conscious beliefs and the prompts we receive from the unconscious, our personalities grow larger. But even though we integrate much that was previously dismissed as evil into our personality, we also encounter values that can never be integrated without destroying our essential being. There is real evil, as the twentieth-century has learned all too well. Ultimate evil can never be fully represented, any more than divinity can. Tolkien is wise enough never to show us Sauron, except through his representatives like Saruman or the Black Riders. And they are terrible enough.

THE SONG OF BEREN & TINÚVIEL

As night falls and fear grows, Strider tells the Hobbits tales of old to lighten their minds. Pressed by Sam to hear more about Elves, Strider chants the story of Beren, son of Barahir and Tinúviel. Though it is a long song, and he only sings part of it, the story line is clear. Beren, a mortal man, sees the Elf-maiden Lúthien dancing in the forest and, enchanted by her beauty, names her Tinúviel (Nightingale in his tongue). The two fall in love and have many adventures. Several times she saves him from danger, but Beren is mortal, and, finally, inevitably, he is murdered and dies in her arms. Grief stricken, Tinúviel rejects her Elven immortality and elects to be mortal, so that eventually she may die and rejoin him. She is the first Elf ever to make this choice and is deeply mourned by the other Elves. But she leaves behind children, who in turn have children, and so on, becoming over time the line of Elves who live among men, though no other rejects their immortality.

Lúthien Tinúviel is the ancestor of Elrond, the father of Arwen Evenstar. And Arwen, like Tinúviel, falls in love with a mortal, and gives up her immortality for that love. And her lover is Aragorn! Thus Aragorn is telling the Hobbits his own tale, a tale that still has hundreds of years to go before its own completion with his death and the later death of his wife and Queen, Arwen Evenstar. And, finally, to close the circle of the tale tightly, it is Arwen who gives up her own passage across the Sea, from Middle Earth to the Havens, to Frodo!

THE BLACK RIDERS REAPPEAR

Soon after Strider finishes telling of Beren and Tinúviel, the Black Riders attack. Strider drives them off, but not before one stabs Frodo in the shoulder, leaving him deathly ill, not merely from the cut, but more from the poison that is part of the knife. At this point in the story, it is beyond Strider's healing abilities to heal Frodo, a marked contrast with what will come later, when he has the healing hands of a king. Strider does what he can with healing herbs, but he knows that they must get Frodo to Elrond in Rivendell if he is to be saved. Unfortunately, Rivendell is still a long way off.

They continue on, with Frodo's condition growing steadily worse. After walking on for another a week, they encounter the Elf Glorfindel, who has been sent from Rivendell to look for them. When he sees the evil markings on the knife that stabbed Frodo, he, too, acknowledges that it is beyond his skill to heal Frodo. In order to save Frodo's strength, he puts him on his own horse, and they advance for another day that way. But then suddenly the Black Riders show up again. Glorfindel tells both Frodo and the horse (who knows better than Frodo what to do) to ride as fast as they can toward Rivendell.

As Frodo clings to the horse in terror, the great horse somehow manages to outdistance the Black Riders and beat them to the Ford that marks the entrance to Rivendell. They cross the Ford ahead of the Riders, but three of the Black Riders enter the stream to follow. When they reach the middle, however, suddenly the river rises and dashes them and their horses off to oblivion.

STRIDER'S TRUE IDENTITY REVEALED

When Frodo awakens, he finds himself in a comfortable bed in Rivendell with Gandalf by his side. They have a long conversation about all that has happened to both since last they met. Since Frodo is most interested in what happened at the Ford to save him, Gandalf explains that Elrond brought off this little piece of magic, though Gandalf admits proudly that he added a little touch: he made the waves take the form of white riders on white steeds (which prefigures Gandalf's own later transformation from Gandalf the Grey into Gandalf the White). He says that Elrond, who is a master healer, was finally able to find a sliver of the poisoned blade buried deep inside Frodo's wound. After that, Frodo began to heal, though as we will later find, he will never fully heal.

Once touched by evil, we can never again be totally free of darkness.

In the course of their talk, Gandalf speaks casually of Aragorn as perhaps the last of the race of the kings who came over the sea as Elf-friends. When Frodo exclaims that "I thought he was only a Ranger,"[99] Gandalf explains that the Rangers are what remains of the Great Men of old, the descendants of Isildur, those who were Elf friends and lived three times as long as normal men. Once Frodo is once again up and about, he learns still more about Aragorn when he overhears Bilbo call Aragorn "Dúnadan." When Frodo asks him what that name means, Bilbo explains that he is "The Dúnadan," which is Elvish for "Man of the West," another reference to his ancestry. And still later, when Frodo sees Aragorn standing deep in conversation with Lady Arwen, he realizes that he is seeing a great lord with his lady, though he has no idea how such a thing can be between a mortal and an Elf.

This is perhaps the time to retreat from the book proper and tell some of the story of Aragorn and Arwen, which Tolkien tells in Appendix A. When Aragorn was two, his father Arathorn was killed by an Orc's arrow at the young age of sixty (well, young for men of his lineage, who normally lived more than two hundred years). Since Aragorn was the Heir of Isildur, he went with his mother to live under the protection of Elrond, who loved him like a son. Since his true identity needed to be concealed for his own protection, he was given still another name, Estel, meaning "hope," for he was the last hope for the line of Men. When he was twenty, Elrond told him his true identity and thereafter called him Aragorn.

> *Aragorn's story has many of the characteristics associated with the birth of the hero in myth and legend. Compare it, e.g., with the story of Moses. At the time of his birth, the Pharaoh had insisted that all male Hebrew babies be killed. In order to protect him, his mother places him in a watertight container and releases him on the Nile. He is found by the Pharaoh's daughter and raised as her son. He is even given a new symbolic name. He only gradually comes to know his real identity. The story of Oedipus in Greek myth has many of the same elements, as do many other stories of heros (tragic in the case of Oedipus). This is everyone's story. We are all born great heros, future kings, but we are each raised under names that others give us. Only gradually do we come to learn our real name, which, as Treebeard explained to Merry and Pippin, is an accumulation of our full life's experience.*

Having found his true identity, Aragorn then found the love of his life. One day, while walking through the woods at sunset, he, like Beren, saw a maiden so beautiful that he thought he was dreaming. He had been singing the song of Lúthien and Beren, and now here Lúthien appeared. So, like Beren, he calls out Tinúviel (nightingale) to her. She laughs and tells him that she is actually Elrond's daughter Arwen, who herself has still another name: Undómiel. When he wonders that he has not seen her in all the years he has lived in Imladris [i.e., Elrond's home], she says that she's been living with her mother and it has been many years since she's lived here. At that, he realizes fully that she is not the young woman she appears, but an Elf princess who has already lived what would be many of his lifetimes. But nevertheless he has fallen in love.

Elrond, who misses little, sees the love in Aragorn's eyes, and with the foreknowledge granted him, tells Aragorn that he is destined to either rise above his ancestors or to fall to the depths. And until he has fulfilled his destiny, he will have no wife. Beyond that, he hopes that Aragorn will not seek Arwen's love, for the line of Elves is greater than that of Men, and someday she must return with her father over the sea to the Havens.

So we see that for heros, there is no halfway measure of success—one must fully fulfill one's destiny. Once we receive a call from within, there is no going back. If we try, we gradually die to life. We have all seen such people.

Accepting his fate, Aragorn leaves to begin the arduous path that leads him toward his fate. Over the next thirty years he conducts his secret battles against Sauron. During those years, he becomes friends with Gandalf, he rides with the Riders of Rohan, fights for the Lord of Gondor, then goes off on his own into the East and the South, looking deep into the souls of men to find those things he needs to find within himself.

There is no quick way to find our fate. Each of us has to take the slow, hard path that leads us ineluctably to the discovery of who we are. That is because the person who we are destined to be has to be chipped gradually out of the hard rock inside us, much as a sculptor creates a work of art.

When he is almost fifty, he wishes to return to Rivendell, but stops first at Lórien, where he finds Arwen visiting Galadriel. Out of his worn Ranger gear and clad in Elven clothing appropriate for the Heir of Isildur, he now appears to Arwen not as the boy she saw previously, but as a man among men, a throwback to greater days, or perhaps a step beyond them into the future of men. And she, too, falls in love, and vows to become his wife, even if it means giving up her immortality.

Many men are satisfied to stay boys all their lives. They attract women who want to mother them. Those women mirror the undeveloped feminine quality within the men. As a man grows and develops, so too does the type of woman who responds to him change. This change reflects the development of the feminine within him, which grows in the unconscious as his masculinity grows consciously. Some men are satisfied to stay at this stage, with their feminine fully carried by a woman without. Only a few men grow still further and integrate both masculine and feminine within.

Though, since Aragorn is the classic male hero, this is described in terms of a man's development, it is no less true for a woman. She, too, can be satisfied to stay at the stage where she never fully separates from her mother (or father). Or she can grow into a woman who can leave the bonds of her parents and relate fully to a man. But only a few go past that point and learn to integrate the masculine within.

Arwen's decision hurts Elrond deeply, but since he still loves Aragorn like a son, he tells him that if this must be, he will accept it—but only if Aragorn fulfills his destiny and becomes the king of both Gondor and Arnor. Only such a man deserves an Elven Queen. After that, they speak no more, and Aragorn returns to his life of wandering and danger. Now many years more have passed, as we return to the chronology of our story at the Council of Elrond.

At the Council, Boromir rises proudly to tells first of the dire situation in Minas Tirith, the capital city of Gondor. He then reveals that he was driven to seek Imladris because of a dream. His younger, but wiser, brother Faramir had the dream first, and it reoccurred to him many times. But it came also once to Boromir. In the dream, a great black storm is coming from the East, while in the West there is still a faint light shining. A voice comes from the West crying "seek for the Sword that was broken."[100] The dreams says that the Sword will be found in Imladris, where a great council will take place, and proof will be given of the approaching doom. Finally the voice concludes: "For Isildur's Bane shall waken. And the Halfling forth shall stand."[101] "Isildur's Bane" is the name given by the Men of the West to the Ring cut from Sauron's finger, and the Halfling, is, of course, Frodo.

After having this dream, Faramir wanted to come to Imladris, but typically, the arrogant Boromir thought that the journey would be dangerous and went himself. When he stops speaking, Aragorn stands and throws his sword on the table, identifying it as the Sword that was Broken! Boromir has no idea what to make of this hard, dark man in worn clothing (for Aragorn is once more dressed as Strider), and asks what this has to do with Minis Tirith. Elrond then explains just who Aragorn is, including the fact that he is Isildur's descendent. This is still one more revelation for Frodo, who jumps up and tells Aragorn that, therefore, the Ring should be his. Aragorn gently explains that the Ring belongs to no one, but it is Frodo's to carry for a time. At that, Frodo brings out the Ring for all to see.

Upon seeing the Halfling (Frodo) and Isildur's Bane (the Ring), Boromir, who can never think any further than his beloved Minis Tirith, immediately interprets the dream to mean that Gondor's doom is at hand. Aragorn points out that the world is bigger than Minis Tirith, and that while dark times approach, those are the times when heros can accomplish great deeds. He explains further that "The Sword that was Broken" is that of king Elendil, which was broken when he fell at Sauron's feet, just before his son Isildur cut the Ring from Sauron's hand. And he asks Boromir if he wants the "House of Elendil" (hence Aragorn) to return to Gondor (i.e., to return with the Sword to help defend Gondor.) Boromir is too proud to accept any help, and certainly too proud to admit that perhaps Aragorn might be the king that the Stewards of Gondor have awaited for so long.

Originally "Steward" was an honorary title given to the chief counselor of the king of Gondor. But after the last king died, the Stewards came to rule Gondor. Though their role was to simply hold the kingdom in trust for the king, no matter how long that might take, over time they came to regard themselves as kings. By the time our story takes place, neither Denethor nor Boromir has any intention of recognizing the real king, even if he does appear, as Aragorn has now appeared before Boromir.

Aragorn, as always, is quiet and modest in response to Boromir's doubts. He tells Boromir that he knows that his appearance belies his claim to be a king, but that's because his life has been hard and filled with wandering. He and his Rangers have played every bit as important a part in the defense against the enemy, as has Gondor. And, while those who defend Minis Tirith have been accorded the grandeur that such heroism deserves, the Rangers have been feared and avoided by the very people they help. Yet Aragorn feels that even this is as it should be, since simple people need to live simple lives, free from the worries they would have if they knew the extent of evil in the world. But now he knows that the Cold War has ended and the real War has begun. It is time for him to take on his appointed role: he will, indeed come to Gondor.

But there is a long way to go before he and Boromir must part from the rest of the Company of the Ring. Until then, he will serve as the second-in-command behind Gandalf. Before he leaves, the Elves use their skills as blacksmiths to reforge the Sword that was Broken. Aragorn names the newly joined sword Andúril, Flame of the West. But other than that piece of majesty, he leaves Imladris as he came, clad only as a Ranger.

In the contrast between Boromir and Aragorn, we see the difference between one who deserves to be king and one who, though strong and brave, never develops the wisdom and humility which are indispensable attributes of a king.

A LEADER GROWS TOWARD HIS DESTINY

Though we see many of Aragorn abilities displayed as the Company proceeds forward under Gandalf's direction, it is only when Gandalf falls from the bridge of Khazad-Dûm that he begins to slowly take on the mantle of the leader he will become. Sick at heart over Gandalf's death, he nevertheless takes immediate charge of the company, which is badly in need of leadership. Though there is little hope without Gandalf, he says grimly: "we must do without hope."[102] He then leads the company to Lothlórien, where they find succor for a time.

When they leave Galadriel's kingdom, Aragorn is unsure which direction to take. He had originally planned to go with the Company until they came to a place where he and Boromir must part from them and go to Minis Tirith. But, with Gandalf dead, he is torn between his vow to help defend Minis Tirith and his need to provide leadership for the rest of the Company. Yet there is still a way to go before the two roads must necessarily part. So they board Elvish boats and go down the Great River until they come to the Argonath: two great stone statues of kings that loom over the river like gods. The sight is so impressive that all, save Aragorn (and of course Legolas, who fears nothing), are cowed and look away in fear. Aragorn tells them not to be afraid, for these great statues are his ancestors: Isildur and Anárion. When Frodo looks over at his friend, he no longer sees the tired, rough figure of the Strider he has come to know so well, but instead "a king returning from exile to his own land."[103]

Often those on the path toward self-realization are given moments of grace when they see their destiny before them. The path is long and hard and such glimpses of the light help sustain us on our journey.

What happens when they leave their boats and come ashore has already been discussed from other points of view in earlier chapters: Boromir tries to steal the Ring, lies to Aragorn about what has happened, then, on his death bed, Boromir confesses and asks for forgiveness. As is so characteristic of Aragorn the leader, he has no words of criticism for Boromir, only praise for the victory he has accomplished. Since there is no physical victory that has occurred—Frodo and Sam off on their own, Merry and Pippin captured by Orcs—Aragorn is praising Boromir for his victory over his own limitations. Aragorn blames himself for what has happened to split the company. He is desperately afraid that he has failed, and Gandalf was wrong to trust him as the leader.

This is the low point for Aragorn because he struggles with the fear that he, like Isildur, will not rise to the level of what a leader must be. And now he feels that already he has failed. Yet, typical of a great man, while most would have placed the blame on Boromir, Aragorn blames only himself.

Aragorn is a leader, and leaders must take charge, regardless of the depths of their despair. First must come as dignified a funeral as is possible for Boromir under the circumstances. Aragorn, Legolas and Gimli place Boromir in one of the Elven boats, then push it out into the river, where it sails over the Falls of Rauros, to be lost forever. Lost but not unnoticed; later we find that his funeral journey is seen in a vision by his prescient brother Faramir. Afterwards, there are two possible paths open before the company: attempt to follow Frodo and Sam, or try to rescue Merry and Pippin from the Orcs. Aragorn once more makes the decision. He realizes that Frodo's path has diverged from the rest of the company, and that they cannot help him further. Though the chances are slim, perhaps they can still save Merry and Pippin. So he leads Legolas and Gimli on their legendary run after the young Hobbits.

Despite his self-doubts, Aragorn takes command and makes a choice. Leaders don't run away from decisions.

When after nearly four days of running, they are confronted by the Riders of Rohan, under the leadership of Éomer, Aragorn's tact gets them past a sticky initial situation. Then, knowing time is short, Aragorn for the first time proclaims his full majesty. He pulls forth his newly forged sword, Andúril, and declares proudly: "I am Aragorn, son of Arathorn, and am called Elessar, the Elfstone, Dúnadan, the heir of Isildur Elendil's son of Gondor. Here is the Sword that was Broken and is forged again! Will you aid me or thwart me? Choose swiftly!"[104]

Frodo was the first of the company to see the king in Aragorn: a glimpse when he stood with Arwen in Rivendell, then again when they sailed past the Argonath. Now Legolas and Gimli see their companion transformed from the Strider they know into someone far greater. His majesty is too much for Éomer, who steps back in confusion, then gives them the horses they need and allows them to go on about their business.

Here we have a foreshadowing of greatness. Again, in each of our lives, if we are willing to do the slow, hard work it takes to find our myth, such intimations of greatness occur. And others around us are awed by the person who is thus revealed. for we all have such majesty inside.

Later, when Gandalf appears, transmogrified into Gandalf the White, he tells Aragorn not to regret his choice of following Merry and Pippin rather than Frodo and Sam. Though the cunning of the young Hobbits and the protection of Treebeard means the Hobbits are no longer in danger, this path brought him to Gandalf, who now asks him to accompany him to Rohan. The two face each other, one a king awakened to his calling, the other a wizard now without equal in the world. And the king is wise enough to recognize that it is not yet time for him to command. He bows graciously to Gandalf's request and once more becomes second-in-command.

We see still another glimpse of Aragorn's greatness during the defense of Helm's Deep. While Legolas and Gimli are having their grisly contest to see who can kill the most Orcs, Aragorn rushes from one weak defensive position to another, always arriving just in time to help save the day. But they seem to be fighting a losing battle against superior forces. At dawn, Aragorn stands above the gates and addresses the enemy, who jibe at him, confident in their victory-to-come. But, though everything to this point has gone the Orcs' way, and defeat seems imminent, Aragorn warns them to "Depart, or not one of you will be spared. Not one will be left alive to take back tidings to the North. You do not know your peril."[105] And, for a moment, they are silenced.

As the story develops, Aragorn increasingly is able to awe those around him by the sheer force of his personality. As we develop, we must never run away from our own strength, and confuse it with arrogance. Boromir is arrogant, Aragorn is strong.

Then they laugh and once more bombard the gate. As the gate falls, out from the fortress ride King Théoden and Aragorn, leading their forces, and their joint presence is so overwhelming that the Orcs break and run. But there is no escape, for at that propitious time, Gandalf appears again, leading a thousand foot soldiers. Caught between the pincers, the Orcs die, as Aragorn had warned. And those who manage to flee into the trees of Fangorn die there, for Treebeard and the Ents also have no love of Orcs.

THE KING GATHERS HIS ARMY

The next step in Aragorn's rise to his destiny occurs in the period after Gandalf deals summarily with Saruman at Orthanc, then rides off to Gondor with Pippin. Aragorn, together with Legolas, Gimli, Merry, Théoden and a small company of Théoden's men are on the road back to Rohan when they encounter more than thirty mounted warriors. Fearing still another trick of Saruman's, they are relieved to find instead that the men are Rangers who say that they were summoned by Aragorn! In actuality, the summons was sent by Galadriel, wise Galadriel, who knew that Aragorn needed his kinsmen. She sent word to Rivendell, where Elrond's two sons, Elladan and Elrohir, heard it, rode off to notify the Rangers, then accompanied them. They bring Aragorn two messages, one from Elrond, one from Arwen, each reminding him that little time remains. Elrond, drawing on his foreknowledge of things to come, tells him further: "remember the Paths of the Dead."[106] Along with Arwen's message, which includes an endearment, she has also sent him a tall staff, with a black cloth wrapped around it. Aragorn knows what the black cloth is and leaves it furled for the present.

Aragorn broods over the two messages, then decides what he must do: he looks into the Palantir of Orthanc. This is the seeing stone that Wormtongue injudiciously threw at Gandalf; the stone into which Pippin, with his insatiable curiosity, gazed, there to be trapped by Sauron's frightening eye. But Aragorn, as the descendent of the kings of old, is the proper owner of the Stone, and is too strong for Sauron to capture (though just barely). He uses the Palantir to gather information, but also to let Sauron see that the rightful king has returned; Aragorn even holds forth his newly forged sword, which Sauron recognizes as the sword that, Elendil bore millennia before. In the stone, Aragorn sees terrible trouble approaching Gondor from the South; unless he gets there soon with an army, Gondor will fall. And so his fate is decided: there is no quicker way East than through the Paths of the Dead, and the only army he can raise quickly enough is the Army of the Dead who lie along that Path.

> *Now a legend begins to come to life. Aragorn is able to look at ultimate evil in the person of Sauron, and survive. But note that he can't face Sauron directly. He has to do so through the seeing stone, and still he barely survives. As we grow in our moral development, we must be willing to face deep moral conflicts, but we must also remember that there are powers beyond our own.*

The story of the Army of the Dead is one of betrayed trust. Long ago, when Gondor was first built, the Men of the Mountains swore an oath to Isildur to help defend their joint territories against Sauron if an attack ever came. Yet, by the time of the great battle that ended the Second Age, the Men of the Mountains had fallen under Sauron's sway, and refused to fight against him. Because of their treachery, Isildur put a curse on them: not even death would provide them rest until they fulfilled the oath they had broken. The Men of the Mountains fled to caves beneath the earth and eventually their line died there.

In the three thousand years since, the Dead have lain inside the caverns still bound by the curse. A door remains cut into a mountain in Dunharrow; the nearby villagers say that sometimes the Dead inside the caverns drift like fog through the door and pass down the road. At such times, the villagers hide in their homes. Those foolish enough to force their way inside that door are never seen again, for the Dead will not let anyone living pass through their realm.

Aragorn tells King Théoden his decision, then they part, Théoden to join the troops he left behind in the hills, Aragorn and his companions toward Dunharrow and the entrance to the Paths of the Dead. Meanwhile, Théoden's niece Éowyn has been left in charge of the outpost at Dunharrow. She has fallen in love with Aragorn and so is elated when she sees Aragorn arrive. But her excitement is quickly chilled when he tells her his mission. Still, despite her fear that he is going to his death, she begs Aragorn to let her accompany him. When he reminds her that her duty is to remain behind and guard the home front, she says bitterly: "All your words are but to say: you are a woman and your part is in the house."[107] And when he insists that this is not her path, she says that neither is it the path of the rest of his companions, who accompany him only because they love him. She does not need to add that she, too, loves him. When they part, she will not meet him again until Aragorn appears as king in the Halls of Healing to help heal the wound she suffered in killing the Lord of the Nazgûls.

> *Though Tolkien understands men better than women and usually regards women only from a man's point-of-view, he has glimpses into aspects of women not commonly seen in literature. Though men rarely acknowledge it, a woman such as Éowyn is not that uncommon; there is an Éowyn or a Joan of Arc inside every woman ready to respond to the call.*

The next day, Aragorn leads his company to the dark door that opens into the caves that are the Paths of the Dead. We have already spoken of how even Gimli the Dwarf is uneasy in these dread caves. But not Aragorn (and not Legolas the Elf). After marching in fear for many miles, the company comes to a space so empty that there are no longer walls to be seen on any side. There Aragorn calls forth the dead, summoning them to follow him into battle. Suddenly all the company's torches go out; while the company had been frightened before, now they are terrified. The rest of their journey is made in total darkness, with the dead rising from their graves and following behind.

Aragorn is able to pass through the caves of the dead because he has faced the darkness within his own soul. Legolas, as an Elf, as an immortal, has no fear of death. Gimli, though now set on the right path through Galadriel's love, has not yet progressed as far as Aragorn.

Once out of the caves, Aragorn urges them all, both living and dead, on to greater speed, racing to reach before day's end the Stone of Erech: a huge black stone buried in the earth. The part that remains above ground is perfectly round and as tall as a man. The fields about it are where the Dead gather for council among themselves once they have emerged from their caves. When Aragorn's company arrives at the Stone, he blows upon a silver horn, then cries out to the Dead, asking why they have come. A voice answers: "To fulfil our oath and have peace."[108] Aragorn then tells him that their time has finally come. If they follow him and rid the land of Sauron's men, their oath will be fulfilled and they can rest in peace. Then he leads them forth, following the living.

For five days, they ride through lands under Sauron's rule. As they pass, the Dead grow stronger and more substantial, until, though still clearly dead, they look more like warriors ready for battle. Any of Sauron's men they encounter along the way flee in terror. Most of those they meet who are not allied with Sauron also flee at the sight of the Army of the Dead, but some brave ones agree to follow Aragorn, but only once the Dead have passed. Aragorn knows that Minas Tirith is already under attack and pushes his army mercilessly. For if they arrive too late, it would be just as well that they had come not at all.

Finally they arrive at the harbor in Pelargir, where fifty great ships are anchored, the largest part of the fleet of the black pirates of Umbar.

Once at the harbor, those who have fled ahead to escape the Dead can go no farther on land and are forced to board the ships. Aragorn calls the host of the Dead into action and they sweep over the enemy, whether on land or sea. They have no need to kill with their swords for the enemy is so terrified that they leap from the ships, leaving only chained slaves behind. Aragorn then puts one of his Rangers in command of each ship. They free the slaves and offer them a chance to fight as free men against the enemy who has enslaved them.

Finally, Aragorn turns to the Dead and tells them that their oath is fulfilled; they may now go in peace. At that command, they seem to melt away, as if they had never been there.

If we are brave enough to take the journey within, ultimately the darkness inside us does dissolve and fade away in the light.

With the Dead gone and the enemy routed, many men, both those just freed and other from the nearby territories, gather around Aragorn, ready to fight against Sauron. They board the ships and Aragorn sails forth with his fleet, hoping he will arrive before Minas Tirith falls.

The greatest single battle that occurs in *The Lord of the Rings* is the battle of Pelennor Fields, which surround Minas Tirith, the capital of Gondor. As we saw in earlier chapters, while the battle rages, Denethor, the Steward of Gondor, ignores the needs of his people and instead tries to immolate himself and his son Faramir. In order to prevent this, Gandalf, who has taken charge of the defense in the absence of Denethor and Faramir, is diverted from the battle at a crucial time. The forces of Rohan, under the leadership of King Théoden, have come to Gondor's aid and are fighting in the fields. When Théoden is slain by the Lord of the Nazgûls, his niece Éowyn and Merry together manage to kill the seemingly invincible Black Rider, thus putting fear into the hearts of his men. But still the battle would have been lost; Sauron's forces are simply too numerous and too powerful.

At this critical point, Aragorn arrives from over the sea with his flotilla of ships. Since each ship carries a black pirate flag, initially the enemy cheers and the forces of Gondor and Rohan fall silent. But then all see, on the lead ship, a great black banner waving—the banner Arwen created for Aragorn. Centered on the banner is a White Tree, representing Gondor's ties to past greatness. Once, for many years such a tree bloomed in the fountain in the center of Minas Tirith, but the tree has stood barren for many years. Around the tree are sewn jewels representing the stars in the black sky, and a crown fashioned of mithril and gold looms above the tree. These symbols have neither been worn nor displayed by anyone since the days of Elendil, Isildur's father, the last king to unite both the kingdoms of Arnor and Gondor.

When one fully takes on one's destiny, often some symbolic gesture is necessary. Our new identity has to have an outer expression. And what more appropriate that a White tree on a black background, showing the light that emerges out of the darkness.

The forces of Gondor and Rohan are revitalized by this unexpected aid, and the enemy is disheartened; it is as if, in the blink of an eye, friend has turned into foe. Still the enemy stands and fights, and the battle rages hotly for many hours. But they are now fighting a losing battle; at the end of the day, Minas Tirith still stands, and there is no enemy left alive.

THE HEALING HANDS OF THE KING

After the battle is won, it is time to deal with the dead and wounded. Among the wounded are Faramir and Éowyn and Merry, as we saw in the chapter on the Path of Curiosity. Though the healers of Gondor are well versed in leechcraft, they have no idea how to help these three, since they are afflicted with the Black Shadow, an illness caused by the Black Riders. Those affected invariably fade into an ever deeper coma, then into catatonia, and finally death. The eldest of the women who serve in the House of Healing weeps and cries out that if only there were a king in Gondor they could be healed, for it is written that "the hands of the king are the hands of a healer."[109] At that, Gandalf goes out to find Aragorn, the rightful king of Gondor.

But Aragorn is not yet ready to proclaim his kingship; that time will come only when Sauron has been defeated. Though they have won a major battle at great cost, it is but a skirmish when one considers

Sauron's massive forces. Nevertheless, at Gandalf's urging he comes to the hospital, wearing no trappings of majesty save the green stone given him by Galadriel. The first person who greets him there is Pippin, for whom Aragorn is still simply old friend Strider. When others who have fought beside Aragorn as their leader are upset that he is called by such a common name, Aragorn tells them that, when he is king, he will make Telcontar—Elvish for Strider—the name of his house.

A reminder that, though Aragorn now seems great and powerful, he is still the same friend that the Hobbits knew as Strider. This is only possible if we have fully integrated all the aspects of our life into a single inviolable whole.

He goes to the rooms of Faramir, Éowyn, and Merry and examines each in turn. Their condition looks grave and he says that he wishes that Elrond was there, for his is the greatest healing power. But Elrond is not there, only Aragorn, whose healing powers we saw earlier were not enough to help Frodo when afflicted by the Black Shadow. But times have changed. Aragorn asks those present in the hospital if among the herbs of healing they have any athelas, which is also called kingsfoil. Though the nurses have none available, they know which herb he means and go to seek it in the fields. While they are off, the herbmaster of the house arrives and tries to display his erudition, giving all the learned terms for kingsfoil, then adding that the herb has no use, unless you believe old wive's tales. Gandalf loses his patience and tells him then to find someone less erudite who still keeps the herb.

Meanwhile, Aragorn holds his hand on Faramir's forehead and calls him gently to return to life. Those in the room can see a great strain upon Aragorn as he does this. Someone rushes into the room carrying leaves of athelas, but fears that they might not serve as they were plucked more than two weeks earlier. Aragorn smiles and reassures him; he has already managed to pull Faramir back from the dead. He crushes the leaves, then throws them into waiting bowls of steaming water. The fragrance fills the air and lightens the mood of those in the room. When Aragorn holds the steam before Faramir's face, Faramir stirs, then wakens. He gazes up at Aragorn and says: "My lord, you have called me. I come. What does the king command."[110] Aragorn tells him to rest more, but to stay awake, then eat when he feels up to it. When Aragorn leaves the room, the others realize, if they hadn't already, that the king has at last returned to Gondor.

Aragorn goes next to Éowyn. He feels the cold in the arm that struck the Nazgûl down. But he also sees that there is a coldness in Éowyn that predates this encounter. When he turns to her brother Éomer to ask about this, Éomer says that he was not aware of any such coldness until Aragorn arrived in their kingdom the first time. Gandalf will have none of this, and reminds Éomer that she was a warrior borne into the body of a woman. While he had battles to fight and freedom to roam, she was forced to perform a woman's duties for a king caught under the spell of Wormtongue. At this, Éomer grows silent.

But Aragorn knows what Éomer meant. He tells him that it is a terrible thing for a man to feel a woman's love and not be able to return it. He can heal her body, but not her heart, which is what is keeping her in the darkness. At that, he leans down, kisses her on the forehead, and calls for her to waken. She begins to breathe more deeply. Then he crushes two more leaves of kingsfoil into steaming water, and uses the water to bathe her forehead and her cold arm. Then, once again he calls for Éowyn to wake. He asks Éomer to hold her hand and wake her. As Aragorn leaves the room, Éowyn finally wakes.

By the time Gandalf and Pippin come to Merry's room, Aragorn has already called him back from the dead, though he has not yet woken him. When once more he crushes the leaves and calls his name, Merry wakens. Typical of a Hobbit, the first thing he says is that he's hungry.

Though the concept of the king as healer has precedent in myth and legend, it has probably never had better expression. Jungian psychology talks of the "wounded healer" who is able to heal others because he has already faced the same problems within himself. Aragorn could not heal the black shadow within Frodo when he was stabbed by the Black Riders because he had not yet progressed far enough in his own development. Now he has.

ARAGORN THE KING

In the previous chapter, we told of how Aragorn and Gandalf came to the Black Gate outside Mordor with their small body of men, and of Gandalf's defiance of Sauron. But this was a battle to be won not by force or arms, but by Frodo's completion of his task (with help from Sam and even Gollum). Since this chapter concerns Aragorn and the Path of the king, let us pass on to when he finally becomes king of the reunited kingdoms of Gondor and Arnor.

You will recall the history of Gondor: the Stewards had given up hope that the king would ever return and had themselves usurped the powers of a king. With Denethor now dead by his own hand, and Faramir healed, Faramir is now the Steward of Gondor. But Faramir, both wiser and humbler than Denethor or Boromir, recognizes Aragorn as the king for whom the Stewards have waited so long. It is time for Aragorn to be crowned king.

The people of Minas Tirith line the streets on the day of his coronation. The flag of the Stewards flies over the city for one last time. Though the great gate of the city has been destroyed during the battle of Pelennor, a temporary, symbolic barrier has been erected, before which stands Faramir the Steward. The remaining forces of the West, those who fought so bravely with Aragorn, march to the city, then line up outside it, leaving a space for their leaders to pass. Aragorn comes forth, dressed simply but as a king, no longer Strider the Ranger. He is accompanied by Éomer of Rohan, Prince Imrahil of Dol Amroth (who fought with Aragorn, but who we have not discussed), Gandalf, and the four Hobbits.

The crowd buzzes at the sight of these great figures, and perhaps even more at the Hobbits. Already Frodo's tale has been told and distorted into a form that can be understood by all: the rumors are that, tiny as he is, he fought with Sauron himself. And, of course, in a way that they would find hard to understand, so Frodo did fight with Sauron. But it is Aragorn above all that their eyes are upon, and their name for him is that given by Galadriel: Lord Elfstone. Word of both his success in arms and his healing hands has spread widely.

Faramir comes forth, kneels before Aragorn, holds out the white rod symbolic of his office and says: "The last Steward of Gondor begs leave to surrender his office."[111] Aragorn takes the rod, then hands it back. Though the king has returned, he still needs a Steward, as did his ancestors before him. Faramir and his heirs are to remain Stewards of Gondor, as long as Aragorn and his heirs rule. Faramir then stands and announces Aragorn's lineage and titles, and asks the symbolic question of the crowd: should he be allowed to enter the city and become king. And there are no dissenters in the cheer that rises up around them.

Though in olden days, the king would crown his successor before he died, that is, of course, impossible in this case. So Faramir takes the crown out of its case and hands it to Aragorn, who holds it up for all to see. He then replaces it and asks Frodo to bring the crown to Gandalf, then Gandalf to place it on his head. And so they do. And when he stands, now crowned as the king, King Elessar, he looks so magnificent that Faramir cries "Behold the king."[112]

And so his reign begins. But in the court of the fountain in the middle of Minas Tirith the symbolic White Tree is still dead. A new symbol is needed for a new age, so one day Gandalf comes and takes Aragorn up to a high place on Mount Mindolluin overlooking the city, a place where traditionally only kings have gone before. There, amidst the snow, where all else is barren, Aragorn sees a small sapling that bears flowers as white as the snow. He carefully removes the little tree from the earth, and brings it back to the city, where it is planted in the place of the dead tree. And once planted, it soon begins to grow and blossom.

In order to be recognized as the king in battle, Aragorn needed the symbolic banner Arwen had created for him. Now, in order to once more start a line of kings that will far outlast him, he needs a living symbol. A tree is a the great traditional symbol of the fully developed personality, which is rooted in the earth of our unconscious instincts, lives in the everyday world, yet stretches up to the heavens for light. The tree that had previously grown in Gondor died long before, symbolizing the death of the line of Gondor's kings. Now a new living tree stands to symbolize a new line of Kings, beginning with Aragorn.

Only one thing more remains for Aragorn: to wed Arwen Evenstar as his Queen. Each of the two great Elven kingdoms comes in force for the wedding, led by their leaders, Galadriel and Celeborn from Lothlórien, Elrond and his two sons Elrohir and Elladan from Rivendell. With both joy and sadness, Elrond gives his daughter's hand in marriage to Aragorn, knowing that in doing so, he is fated to lose her forever.

For one hundred twenty years, they live together as king and Queen. But even for so long-lived a man as Aragorn, long life is not immortality. And so there comes a day when he knows it is his time to die. He goes to the House of the kings and lies there on a bed. He hands his son Eldarion his crown and scepter, then asks to be left alone with Arwen. Arwen, who has lived many human lifetimes before she ever saw Aragorn, asks if he can't stay a little longer with her, but they both know his time has come. He reminds her that she still has a choice: she can go to the Havens and live with her kindred forever. If so, their life together will remain as a memory, bittersweet, but eternal. Or she can stay on earth and suffer the same fate as mortals.

But Arwen's choice has been made long before this. Like Lúthien Tinúviel, she has chosen the love of a mortal and now, even if she would choose to go, there are no ships to take her over the Great Sea. Aragorn has one last promise for her "we are not bound forever to the circles of the world, and beyond them is more than memory. Farewell."[113] And then he dies.

With her love gone, Arwen has nothing left to keep her in Minas Tirith. She leaves Gondor and goes to Lórien, empty now these many years since Galadriel and Celeborn and the other wood Elves left over the sea. There she lives alone through the winter. Just before spring comes, she lies down in the green grove where she and Aragorn first pledged their love…and then dies.

And thus truly ends Aragorn's path, for his path is inseparable from the woman he loved, the immortal who chose her love for him over eternity.

Chapter Five
The Path of Tragic Failure

It might seem strange to include Gollum in our list of heroes, but failure can be as instructive as success, if not more so. The tragic hero of Greek drama was someone of great ability who possessed a flaw that ultimately led to their downfall. Perhaps our modern age requires a role reversal, in which a tragic hero is replaced by a villain whose flaw somehow leads him to accomplish something great.

Like the Greek tragic heroes, Gollum has a single flaw that destroys his entire life: his covetousness for the Ring. Throughout *The Lord of the Rings*, the Ring is the central symbol that dominates all else. Everyone's character is seen through their reaction to the Ring. There are those who, like Gollum, when brought into the Ring's proximity, grow to covet it. For example, the book has hardly begun before we find Bilbo, under the sway of the Ring, accusing Gandalf of trying to steal it from him; yet Bilbo manages to triumph over his greed and gives the Ring to Frodo. As Gandalf later points out to Frodo, Bilbo is the only one who was ever able to give the Ring away, even if he needed Gandalf's prodding to do so. Boromir, filled with hubris, thinks himself a better Ring bearer than Frodo. His arrogance leads to the splitting of the fellowship. But afterwards he realizes his sin and tries to redeem himself by his bravery in defending Merry and Pippin. And, of course, without the fellowship being split, perhaps Frodo would never have accomplished his great task. Even figures as great as Aragorn and Gandalf and Galadriel, know the temptation of the Ring. Each imagines what great things they could accomplish with its power, yet each is wise enough to turn away and leave the Ring to the Ring bearer. In the entire story, only Tom Bombadil is indifferent to the Ring; he sees it as a pretty bauble, but has no desire for it. Bombadil is indifferent not only to the Ring, but to all the goings on in Middle Earth beyond his own domain, in which he reigns supreme, at one with nature.

But Gollum is not indifferent to the Ring; he is consumed by his desire for it. As Gandalf tells Frodo, "he hated it and he loved it, as he hated and loved himself."[114]

This might be the most common problem we all have to face along our path of development. For all of us, there is something - alcohol, drugs, sex, fame, wealth, power - whose appeal is so compelling that it makes us forget who we really are, and who we are intended to become. If we yield to that attraction, eventually we all come to both hate it and love it.

HOW THE RING CAME TO GOLLUM, THEN LEFT HIM

After Isildur cuts the Ring from Sauron's hand, he foolishly keeps it for himself, despite Elrond's pleas to throw it into the volcano Orodruin (more commonly known as Mount Doom). But he doesn't possess it long; within two years, by the side of the Great River, Isildur is killed by Orcs. The Ring falls into the River and drifts to the bottom, where it lies for two thousand four hundred and sixty-one years, until one day, one special day, the Hobbit Sméagol's birthday (or so he claimed), Sméagol and his friend Déagol go fishing in the River. An especially big fish pulls Déagol from his boat down deep into the water. There on the River's bottom, he sees something shiny and grabs it. When he come back up to the surface, he finds he is holding a beautiful golden Ring. When Déagol raises it up in delight, Sméagol so desires the Ring that he kills Déagol and takes it for his own, calling it "my birthday present."

If we are to become the person we are intended to be, we must be willing to struggle with our conscience, to hold a tension between competing desires. Gollum doesn't struggle at all. He immediately chooses the path of the villain without any compunction. Having done so, he finds himself driven ineluctably along a path that will give him few rewards, and much suffering.

Sméagol was born into a powerful Hobbit family, part of what eventually became the Stoor clan, which was ruled by his Grandmother.

These particular Hobbits, unlike our friends from the Shire, live near the River and actually like sailing and swimming and fishing. The young Sméagol, like Merry and Pippin, is more curious about the world than his fellow Hobbits. But, unlike Merry and Pippin, whose curiosity pushes them outward toward the wider world, Sméagol "was interested in roots and beginnings . . . his head and eyes were downward."[115] He is always pulled by the possibility of secrets hidden deep within the earth, more like a Dwarf than a Hobbit. But while Dwarves are practical and make something out of what they find inside the earth; Sméagol merely searches aimlessly, not knowing what he seeks.

Though Tolkien was a scholar of prodigious capacity, he was not an introspective man. He distrusted those who looked too deeply into themselves. Yet, despite that distrust of introspection, over the course of the Quest, each of his heroes (save perhaps sweet Sam) is forced to look deeply into his own nature; each is changed in the process.

Now, under the Ring's influence, this tendency increases. He soon discovers that he becomes invisible when he wears the Ring, which leads him to thieving and other villainies. Suspicious of all around him, desirous only of his own company and the company of the Ring, he takes to making strange gurgling sounds in his throat—sounds like "gollum, gollum,"—as he mutters to himself about "his precious." So Sméagol becomes Gollum to the other Hobbits, who grow to fear and despise him. Finally, grown sick of Gollum's evil ways, his grandmother exiles him from the clan.

The Ring itself begins to isolate Gollum, to take him away from his kin. Just like a drug addict, whose only friend is eventually the needle, Gollum has only the Ring for company. And poor company it is.

As he wanders alone, feeling deeply sorry for himself at his mistreatment by his fellow Hobbits, his tendency to look to the dark rather than the light increases. The light of the sun becomes intolerable, so he wanders more by night than day. Though eventually even moonlight bothers him. When he comes to the Misty Mountains, he thinks to himself that it must be dark and cool underneath the

Mountains. There he could roam on his own and discover the secrets hidden in "roots and beginnings." And so for nearly six hundred years, he lives beneath the Misty Mountains, his life prolonged by the powers of the Ring. Until one day Bilbo appears.

> *Gollum's life, under the spell of the Ring, is reminiscent of Yossarian's friend Dunbar in Joseph Heller's Catch-22. Dunbar thinks he can increase his life-span by making his life as boring as possible. Of course, subjectively, this works: time passes ever more slowly for Dunbar, but only because he lives less and less. Similarly, Gollum's life-span increases enormously, but can we really call it life? Look how much life Mozart and Keats lived in 35 years, how little Gollum has lived in the six hundred years of isolation in the darkness.*

At one point during Bilbo's adventures (which were recorded in The Hobbit) he is forced to escape some Orcs. In doing so, he finds himself lost in the Orc-mines beneath the mountains. There, by chance, he discovers a ring on the floor of the tunnel and hides it in his pocket. Little does he know that this isn't just any golden ring, it is the One Ring that was cut from Sauron's hand by Isildur. With the ring in his pocket, Bilbo continues to hunt for a way out of the mines, but instead he finds himself becoming more and more lost, going ever deeper into the mines. When he can go no lower, he comes to a lake with an island in the middle where Gollum lives.

Gollum has degenerated to such a point that no one would ever recognize him as being a Hobbit. After all this time cut off from the light of the sun, he is totally grey, with large, bulging eyes which help him to see in the darkness. He lives largely on fish, which he eats raw, but he will eat anything that he can easily kill, including Orcs, or even Hobbits. If Bilbo hadn't had his sword Sting in his hand (the very sword that he later gave to Frodo), Gollum would have immediately killed Bilbo. Instead, biding his time, he offers to play a riddle game with Bilbo. If he wins, he will eat Bilbo; if Bilbo wins, Gollum will show him the way out of the mines. This riddle game is a reminder that there is still a Hobbit alive somewhere in Gollum, for Hobbits love riddles and the Riddle game is respected by all creatures.

The Riddle game is Life's attempt to call back Gollum from the depths to which he has sunk. It is a reminder that he was once a Hobbit, and that there are rules that are respected by all. All of us are forced to play a Riddle game at some point in our lives. There comes a series of questions to which we have to supply answers. These questions, which are often moral choices, push us to our limits. If we answer them well, our life expands; if we answer them poorly, our life contracts.

With little alternative, Bilbo accepts the challenge, in the hope that he can somehow defeat Gollum at the game. Both know many riddles, so the game goes on for a long time. Finally, with his stock of riddles exhausted, Bilbo happens to put his hand in his pocket and feels the Ring. He immediately asks Gollum what he has in his pocket. Gollum complains bitterly that this isn't really a riddle, but still he accepts the challenge, only demanding that he have three guesses instead of the usual one. His first guess is very shrewd: "hands." But luckily Bilbo has just removed his hands from his pocket before Gollum's guess. Then Gollum thinks of all the things he might have kept in his pocket and tries "knife." Wrong again. Finally, giving way to despair he guesses: "string, or nothing."[116] While that is technically four guesses, Bilbo hardly objects, since Gollum is wrong on both counts.

But by then, a niggling suspicion is forming at the back of Gollum's mind: where is his precious? He can no longer bear to be parted from his precious. As Bilbo stands, Sting in hand, insisting that Gollum keep his side of the bargain and show him the way out, Gollum says that first he has to check on something. He leads Bilbo to his lair to look for the Ring, and when he finds it is gone, he begins to shriek. He insists that Bilbo tell him what he does have in his pocket. When Bilbo answers that "answers were to be guessed, not given,"[117] the suspicion is strong that this nasty hobbit has stolen his precious. No sword is going to stop Gollum now; he springs at Bilbo who flees in terror from this mad creature.

In his flight, Bilbo's hand goes into his pocket and the Ring slips onto his finger. As we saw with Frodo, first in the Prancing Pony and later on Weathertop, the Ring seems to be able to place itself on people's fingers with little or no action on their part. And so Bilbo becomes invisible, though he doesn't yet know it. When he trips and falls, he expects Gollum to jump on him and kill him. But instead Gollum goes running by, not noticing Bilbo lying on the ground. At first, Bilbo can't figure out why, but as Gollum keeps muttering about the nasty creature who has stolen his birthday present, his precious, he begins to realize that perhaps Gollum's birthday present is the Ring he is wearing, and that it must be a magic ring that makes its wearer invisible.

Afraid that Bilbo will escape, Gollum goes as quickly as possible through a necessarily circuitous route toward the exit, counting which passage to take at each decision point. Finally he comes to a final passage, where he stops, muttering that he can't go further because he'd encounter goblins (the Orcs of *The Lord of the Rings*). Without his Ring of invisibility, he wouldn't be safe. So he crouches like a frog at the entrance, blocking the way.

> *Gollum's whole world has become these dark passages. He cannot let the wider world in, or in this case, let a representative of that wider world, out. Especially not with his Precious. We sometimes come to a point where our life has become sharply circumscribed, cut off from anything new. We will do almost anything to protect ourselves from the new. But, of course, this is hopeless: life will have its way with us, whether we cooperate or not.*

Bilbo has followed him, guessing that he will lead him to the exit, and now he is desperate to get past Gollum. He knows that since he is invisible, he could stab Gollum in his eye and kill him. But compassion stays his hand. It doesn't seem fair to Bilbo to kill such a pathetic creature, one who doesn't even have a sword to defend himself (though, if Bilbo only knew, Gollum hardly needs a sword.) Instead Bilbo makes a mighty leap which barely clears Gollum, then goes running down the corridor, with Gollum shrieking behind him: "Thief, thief, thief! Baggins! We hates it, we hates it, we hates it forever!"[118] Thus Bilbo escapes with the Ring, or perhaps, as Gandalf surmises, the Ring has simply chosen another bearer who might take it further along on its journey back to its creator.

If Bilbo had not had compassion for Gollum, perhaps neither Gandalf nor Sauron would have ever learned of the existence of the Ring. If so, then the entire battle between Sauron's forces and those of the West would have been fought simply on the battle-field, and Sauron would have won. Or, even if somehow both had learned of the Ring, and the Ring had become a factor, certainly Gollum would not have been alive to guide Frodo to Mount Doom. And again Sauron would have won. Small acts of kindness reverberate in ways that we can never predict.

GOLLUM'S HUNT FOR BILBO AND THE RING

After Bilbo leaves with the Ring, Gollum stays in the caverns, muttering in self-pity about the thief Baggins who has stolen his birthday present. But, though his desire for the Ring never dampens, away from its vampire-like presence, he finds himself growing stronger again. After a year or two, his renewed strength, coupled with his desire to recover his precious from the thief Baggins, is enough to drive Gollum out from his caves beneath the Misty Mountains, into the world he so despises. Traveling largely by dark of night to avoid both sunlight and moonlight, he spends more than six decades in his search for Bilbo. Deprived of the rats in his caves who have been his chief source of food, he kills anything young or weak he finds, often drinking its blood, leaving horror stories in his wake of a new terror that stalks in the night.

Though all Gollum can think of is his loss of the Ring, in its absence, he regains his strength. When we are cut off from whatever "fix" has taken over our lives, we do regain our strength, even if we don't notice it or appreciate it.

Meanwhile, after hearing Bilbo's self-serving story of how he acquired the Ring from Gollum, Gandalf wants to know more about Gollum and how he acquired the Ring. Gandalf searches for him, and sends wood-Elves to search. But Gollum eludes them all and Gandalf, to his later regret, turns to more pressing matters. After all, he still believes Sauron's story that the Ring is irretrievably lost. So for fifty years or more, Gollum is left without interference in his own search for Bilbo. Only later, after Bilbo's birthday party, does Gandalf realize the importance of the Ring, and begins to hunt once more in earnest for Gollum. And this time, he enlists the aid of Aragorn, the greatest hunter of his age, who from his own wanderings, knows every highway and byway of Middle Earth.

Unfortunately, both for Gollum and for Gandalf, Gollum's search eventually brings him too close to Sauron's stronghold in Mordor, where he is caught, taken to Sauron, and tortured to find out what he knows. Sauron finds that Gollum did have a ring of power and, by elimination, Sauron concludes that it was the One Ring. Beyond that, all he can get from Gollum is "Baggins" and "The Shire," but that is enough for Sauron to set the Black Riders off to seek a Baggins in the Shire, wherever that may be. (For, by this time in history, so little knowledge does the rest of the world have of hobbits that neither name means anything to Sauron.) Having finished his interrogation of Gollum, Sauron, ever mindful of using any foul creature for his needs, releases him. He knows that Gollum's own desire for the Ring is so great that, if anyone can find the Ring, it might well be Gollum. If so, there will then be time enough for Sauron to once more reel Gollum in.

> *So the wheels are set in motion that will lead, ineluctably to the destruction of the Ring on Mount Doom, and to Sauron's downfall. Gollum, the villain, is an integral cog in a process bigger than his personal life.*

Gollum then resumes his search for Bilbo, little knowing that he in turn is being hunted. And the hunter eventually finds his prey. Aragorn brings the whining Gollum to Gandalf for questioning. Getting little of use from Gollum, Gandalf eventually has to turn to at least the threat of torture by fire, if not to torture itself, to extract the history of Gollum's acquisition of the Ring, his loss of the Ring to Bilbo, his hunt for Bilbo and the Ring, and his capture by Sauron, who he speaks of indirectly as a powerful friend. And thus Gandalf at last knows the whole story.

He then leaves Gollum to be kept prisoner by the Elves. They prove too tender-hearted for their task and Gollum manages to escape and continue his hunt for the Ring. At this point, he has no idea yet that the Ring has passed on to another hobbit: Frodo.

HOW GOLLUM ONCE MORE BECOMES SMÉAGOL

Somehow—perhaps simply the call of the Ring is enough—Gollum manages to follow Frodo and his companions. As early as the ferry ride toward Buckland, Sam and Frodo notice a small dark figure following their party. On the journey to Lórien, Frodo spots strange eyes in the darkness. And while lying at night on a sleeping platform high up in the trees of Lórien, both Frodo and the Elf Haldir are aware of some unknown creature in the night. Later, when the company have left Lórien and are sailing along the Great River, Sam spots what looks like a log with eyes. That night, Sam and Frodo take turns keeping watch on their boat. Just as Frodo is almost yielding to sleep's call, Gollum grabs the edge of the boat, preparing to board it, and probably try to steal the Ring from Frodo. But when Frodo sees him and draws Sting, Gollum slips back into the water. This is enough to waken Aragorn, who tells Frodo that Gollum has been following them since Moria. Though they will never know for sure, it may not have been Pippin's carelessness that alerted the Orcs in Moria, but Gollum's treachery. We certainly find repeatedly that Gollum is not to be trusted.

But Gollum remains a boogie in the night until the fellowship is broken and Sam and Frodo are on their own, climbing the hills of Emyn Muil, on their way to Mordor. After managing a perilous descent down a steep cliff (which we'll discuss more in the next chapter), Sam hopes that at least they've left Gollum behind. But just then, they see him climbing head-first down the sheer cliff face with his fingers and toes splayed out, "finding crevices and holes that no hobbit could ever have seen or used."[119] Their feelings of repugnance at the sight echo those of Jonathan Harker in *Dracula*:

But my very feelings changed to repulsion and terror when I saw the whole man slowly emerge from the window and begin to crawl down the castle wall over the dreadful abyss, face down with his cloak spreading out around him like great wings. At first I could not believe my eyes. I thought it was some trick of the moonlight, some weird effect of shadow, but I kept looking, and it could be no delusion. I saw the fingers and toes grasp the corners of the stones, worn clear of the mortar by the stress of years, and by thus using every projection and inequality move downwards with considerable speed, just as a lizard moves along a wall.[120]

> *At no point does Gollum seem more inhuman (or in his case, less of a hobbit) than here. To Frodo and Sam, it is as if they were observing a rat scuttling down a wall, or perhaps something lower on the evolutionary scale, some enormous insect. But just as Dracula was once a human, Gollum was once a hobbit, and Frodo is gradually able to touch the hobbit that still lives in Gollum.*

Sam is fed up with being followed by Gollum and decides to turn the tables on him. Gollum reaches a point near the bottom of the cliff, where the cliff is undercut and he can't hold on any longer. He tries to turn around so that his feet face the ground, but he loses his grip and simply falls. The moment he hits the ground, Sam jumps on him. But we see just how strong and resourceful Gollum is, for he manages to wrap his own arms and legs around Sam and squeeze him tighter and tighter. His fingers reach for Sam's throat while he bites into his shoulder. Thankfully, Frodo is there with his sword Sting, or Sam might have been a goner. He pulls Gollum off Sam and shows him Sting, reminding him that he has seen it before. If Gollum had any doubt that this hobbit was connected to Bilbo Baggins, who he hates forever, this removes that doubt.

In a flash, Gollum changes from ferocity to whining and pleading. "Don't hurt us! Don't let them hurt us, precious! They won't hurt us will they, nice little hobbitses? We didn't mean no harm, but they jumps on us like cats on poor mices, they did, precious. And we're so lonely, *gollum*. We're be nice to them, very nice, if they'll be nice to us, won't we, yes, yess."[121]

As Sam and Frodo debate what to do with him, Frodo remembers when he stood by the fire with Gandalf, looking at the Ring and knowing for the first time what it was. Gandalf told him the story of Bilbo and Gollum, and Frodo, in his fear, insisted that Bilbo should have killed Gollum while he had the chance. Gandalf, wiser than Frodo, told him then that "It was Pity that stayed his hand. Pity, and Mercy: not to strike without need."[122] But Frodo has come a long way since then, and no longer feels so sure of his moral rectitude. Sam's values are simpler; he has no pity for Gollum. When he suggests tying him up and leaving him, which would be tantamount to killing him, Frodo says that they can't do that. "Poor wretch! He has done us no harm."[123] Instead he shocks Sam by telling Gollum directly that they are going to Mordor, and he will have to lead them. Since he prefers to travel by the dead of night, when even the moon doesn't shine, they decide to first rest for a bit.

Sam and Frodo see Gollum differently. Sam sees him through realistic eyes and knows he's a villain and not to be trusted. Frodo sees past the creature Gollum has become to the hobbit he once was, and might be again. We all have to find the right balance between justice and mercy.

But mercy is not the same as stupidity. Frodo and Sam sit on each side of Gollum, and pretend to fall asleep. Gollum waits until their breathing lengthens, then tries to leap away into the darkness. But Sam and Frodo are on him like a flash. Now sure just how little he can be trusted, Sam ties an Elven rope around Gollum's foot. But when Gollum starts to shriek in pain, they know this isn't play-acting on his part. Gollum has somehow gone so far into the dark side of things that he can't tolerate anything connected with Elves, who are the living embodiment of light.

A telling incident. If we go too deep into the dark, we can't tolerate the light. We have to slowly work our way back.

So what are the hobbits to do? Frodo realizes that there is only one oath that Gollum can swear that he won't easily break. Gollum knows, too, and says that he will wears on his Precious. As he says this, he calls himself Sméagol, and so Gollum takes the first step back to the hobbit he once was. The creature who scuttled head-first down the cliff face like an insect, recovers a little of his old identity. Though even here, he first tries a little duplicity, wanting to touch his Precious, for surely he knows by now that Frodo has it.

Frodo tells him sternly "No! not on it. . . . Swear by it, if you will. For you know where it is. Yes, you know Sméagol. It is before you."[124]

Before him in the person of Frodo. And Frodo grows in stature before Sam's eyes, just as Gandalf has done standing before Bilbo, just as Aragorn has done standing before the riders of Rohan. At this moment, Frodo has begun fully to move into his destiny.

> *Gandalf and Aragorn and Frodo! Frodo is indeed in good company. Who would have guessed, when we first saw the simple, pleasure-loving hobbit Frodo back in the Shire, that, when put to the test, he could grow to heroic proportions. As the story proceeds, we will see Frodo continue to grow in moral stature, until arguably, he surpasses all others, including Gandalf and Aragorn.*

Sméagol almost falls over himself vowing by the Precious to be good and serve his master well. At that point, Frodo tells Sam to remove the rope from Gollum's leg. When Sam does so, albeit reluctantly, Gollum transforms. He is neither the vicious creature who has been hunting them, nor the whining self-pitying one-time hobbit who begged for his life. Now he is almost friendly, though he still shrinks away from any physical touch. Frodo has become the center of his life: a kind word makes him dance with joy, the mildest reprimand drives him to tears. While Sméagol seems a different character from the Gollum they know, Sam remains as suspicious as ever. "If possible [he] liked the new Gollum, the Sméagol, less than the old."[125] The old Gollum he terms "slinker", the new Sméagol is "stinker."

> *We can certainly sympathize with Sam's view, but, nevertheless, Sméagol is different than Gollum. Some trace of the hobbit inside has truly come to the surface.*

SMÉAGOL THE GUIDE

Now that Sméagol has accepted Frodo as the Master of the Ring, he seems eager to act as their guide. In his search for the Ring, he learned hidden ways into Mordor, that, for a long time, kept him out of the hands of Sauron's Orcs. Moving by dark of night, he leads Frodo and Sam away from the hills and down toward the Dead Marshes that lie between Emyn Muil and Mordor. It is no longer a situation of the hobbits holding

Gollum captive; he moves so fast that he could leave them behind easily at any time. The hobbits are hard pressed simply to keep up with him.

In each of our individual journeys, we must at some point look to the darkness to find our guide.

After a hard night's walk, they stop, exhausted and hungry. Though the hobbits have only the Elves' lembas left to eat, and only about three weeks worth of that, Frodo offers to share it with Sméagol. He sniffs at the leaves from Lórien in which the enchanted waybread is wrapped, and pulls back as if he had smelled something vile. Then when he nibbles on a tiny piece of the lembas, he immediately spits it out and begins coughing as if it had poisoned him. "You try to choke poor Sméagol. Dust and ashes. He can't eat that. He must starve."[126] But immediately, in his new oily Sméagol way, he reassures them that he doesn't blame them. He'll simply have to starve. For Sam, who despises Sméagol even more than he did Gollum, the lembas tastes especially good now he's found that Sméagol can't stand it.

Gollum can only be nourished by things that live in the dark. Anything associated with the light tastes like ashes to him.

When they bed down for the night, Sam tells Frodo that he'll take first watch in case Gollum tries to kill them while they sleep. Frodo reassures him that they have no worries—at least for now—but that Sam should wake him anyway for the second watch. Then Frodo falls deeply asleep, as does Gollum. Sam sits, determined to protect his master, but the night's journey has been long and he falls asleep on his watch, only waking up after sleeping through the entire day. He finds Frodo still asleep, happily unhurt, but Gollum is gone. Sure he has left them, Sam looks up and sees Gollum standing in the near distance. When he tells him to come back, Gollum tells Sam that he's hungry, then leaves.

Sam's yells at Gollum to come back finally wake Frodo. Though Sam apologizes for falling asleep on his watch, Frodo reassures him, saying that they both needed the sleep, and that for now Gollum isn't their worry. A little later, Gollum returns, with his hand and face covered with mud, still chewing, as if he's been grubbing away at things they prefer not to even think about. Then it's time to resume their journey—down into the stinking marshes that surround Mordor.

> *Here, in contrast to the airy-light lembas of the Elves, we see Gollum's disgusting food. Yet sometimes, we all have to eat filth. If we don't swallow some of the darkness, integrate it into our personalities, we are always in danger of being overwhelmed by it. Remember Harry Haller, the reclusive professor in Hermann Hesse's Steppenwolf, who is caught in a tension of opposites between the bourgeois world he professes to despise, and the world of sensuality, represented by a jazz saxophone player (picture a rock star today).*

From here on, there is little point in whether the hobbits trust or distrust Gollum/Sméagol, since they are at his mercy. Once they descend into the mists that cover the swamps, the two hobbits are totally lost. When Frodo asks if there isn't some other way to go, Sméagol tells him in his own oblique way, that of course there are, many ways, and each will bring them to Sauron much more quickly than they would like. "Follow Sméagol very carefully, and you may go a long way, quite a long way, before He catches you, yes perhaps."[127]

> *Only someone who knows the darkness can lead us through the darkness. Only because of Frodo's compassion is Gollum willing to be that guide. It is wise to keep this in mind in our own dealings with the darkness inside us, the darkness of the unconscious.*

And so they move on, with Gollum leading the way, followed by Sam, with Frodo lagging behind in the rear. By this point Frodo is so dragged down by the weight of the Ring that he can hardly move. A more gloomy land is almost unimaginable. By the end of the third day with Gollum, they are in the thick of the Dead Marshes, and soon discover where the name comes from. As they walk in the dark, they see dim lights appearing over the marsh. Gollum tells them that they must keep moving and not look at the lights. But when Sam trips and falls with his face next to the surface of the water, he sees, to his horror, dead faces staring up at him out of the water. Gollum laughs at Sam's distress, telling him that the Dead Marshes got their name, from all those—Elves, Men, and Orcs—who died at the great battle that took place three thousand years ago, at the end of the Second Age, when Isildur cut the Ring from Sauron's hand. And again Gollum warns them to move slowly and carefully and not to look at the lights. "Or hobbits go down to join the Dead ones and light little candles."[128]

A frightening scene, where Sam gets a view into death itself. There are places in each of our journeys when we must simply move forward without looking too closely beneath us.

As they move on, Gollum increasingly stops and sniffs the air, to Sam's irritation. When Sam tells him that there is no need to sniff, as the whole place stinks, Gollum says that he smells a change coming in the air, and he doesn't like it. So they continue on. But soon they hear a far-off cry in the air, a cry they've heard before: Black Riders! Gollum is petrified with fear, babbling to himself. When they see a dark shape flying above, they all fall down, almost burrowing into the ground in the hope of escaping the Black Rider's notice. When the Rider has finally passed them, Frodo and Sam get up. Gollum, who knows the cruelty of the Riders even better than Frodo, stays face-down on the ground until forced up, moaning to himself: "Wraiths! Wraiths on wings. The Precious is their master. They see everything, everything. . . . and they tell Him everything. He sees. He knows. Ach, *gollum, gollum, gollum!* [his emphasis]."[129]

A MORAL DEBATE INSIDE GOLLUM/SMÉAGOL

The passage of the Black Rider has reminded Gollum that his fear of Sauron is greater than his momentary loyalty to Frodo. Though, for a while, Frodo's kindness transformed him back into at least a semblance of the hobbit that he once was, now he adopts a phony, falsely friendly tone. Sam notices the change immediately. Gollum keeps glancing over at Frodo whenever he thinks he's undetected. Frodo, by this point, is so pulled down by the terrible weight of the Ring that he is completely unaware of anything around him. So Sam has to watch Gollum even more carefully now, anticipating some evil to come. On the fifth day of their trip with Gollum, they finally leave the Dead Marshes and come to something every more hideous: the slag heaps that were all that remained of the once green country.

> *Tolkien, who loved nature so much, abominated the destruction caused by industrialization. To him, nothing in nature, not even the Dead Marshes could be as sickening as the desolation left by man's greed. In Mordor, which was his portrait of a world destroyed by industrialization, he says: "nothing lived, not even the leprous growth that feed on rottenness. The gasping pools were choked with ash and crawling muds, sickly white and grey, as if the mountains has vomited the filth of their entrails upon the lands about."*[130]

Frodo and Sam are appalled at the sight, knowing that they will have to cross this wasteland. But first they must rest. Sam wakes when he thinks he hears Frodo calling him. But then he sees that Frodo is still asleep with Gollum sitting by his side, talking to himself, as if he were two different people. One person argues that he promised to obey Frodo. The other insists that their only loyalty is to the Ring, the Precious, and the hobbits are taking it to Sauron. The first side says that he promised to obey the Master, meaning Frodo. The other side says if he had the Ring, he would be the Master. The first reminds him how kind Frodo has been, how he took away the Elven rope when he saw it hurt him, and always talks kindly to him. The other side says then don't hurt him, but get the Ring. But he can make the nasty hobbit, Sam, crawl before him. When the first side says again that they mustn't hurt Frodo, the second reminds him that Frodo is a Baggins, like Bilbo.

> *The fact that such a moral argument can go on inside Gollum shows that he has not become totally evil. The fact that the evil side wins the argument shows, unfortunately, that even Frodo's kindness is not enough to save Gollum from himself.*

Then, with the moral dilemma seemingly resolved, so that he no longer owes any allegiance to Frodo, he begins worrying about "Him;" that is, Sauron. Sauron must know about the promises he made to Frodo, and won't forgive him, so Gollum must keep the Ring for himself. Perhaps with the Ring, he will become even more powerful than Sauron.

But for now he has to bide his time, since there are two hobbits and only one of him. Finally he adds "She might help. She might, yes."[131]

Sam has listened with dismay to this whole schizophrenic exchange, following everything, including the references to "He" and "Him" as Sauron, but he has no idea who "She" might be. Soon he will find out, to his dismay! But for now, he is careful not to let Gollum know that he's been overheard. When Frodo wakes they move on again.

A NEW PATH

As they walk through the dusk, twice again they fall to the ground when Black Riders pass overhead. When, by the third time, Gollum is so frightened that he says they can go no further, Frodo turns stern and puts his hand on the hilt of his sword. And so they move on still again. Another night's journey brings them at last to their destination, the Black Gate that is the entrance to Mordor, the Black Gate where a mere three weeks later Aragorn and Gandalf will arrive with their small force of men to face the might of Sauron.

At the sight of the great Gate, with sentinels clearly visible on top, it is clear to Sam that they can go no farther. But Frodo knows only that he must enter Mordor, no matter what. At the thought of losing his Precious to Sauron, Gollum falls all over himself trying to dissuade Frodo, telling him that if he continues, Sauron will have them, and have his Precious. In his anxiety, he slips and begs Frodo to give it to him, that he will take good care of it, and with it take care of the hobbits. But Frodo is adamant: if this is the only way into Mordor, this way he must take, no matter what the consequences.

Gollum then changes his tune still again and begins to talk about another way. Both Sam and Frodo are suspicious, since they are hearing about this alternative path for the first time. Gollum insists that the only reason he's never mentioned it is because they never asked, they simply told him to take them to the Gates of Mordor. Frodo says that Gollum has treated them well to this point. Twice he could have killed them, and yet did not. So now he will trust him a third time. Just as Sam is beginning to fear that Frodo is altogether too trusting, Frodo changes again before their eyes.

Frodo tells Sméagol that he gave himself away when he asked Frodo to give him the Precious. He says that, not only will Sméagol never again have the Precious, he is in terrible danger since he promised on the Precious to obey Frodo. So now if Frodo was to put on the Ring and command him, he would have to do whatever he was told. If he was told to jump off a cliff, that is what he must do. And, in a way, this is what eventually happens to Gollum. Both Sam and Gollum once again see something in Frodo that they have never seen before. Sam has mistaken his kindness to Gollum for weakness, and now he sees that Frodo is greater and more powerful than he had even imagined.

As one grows wise, one grows kind. But one must also occasionally show one's strength.

Gollum, knowing the power of the Ring, is so frightened that for some time, Frodo can get nothing more out of him than whining and begging for his life. Finally, Gollum has calmed down enough to tell of this other way into Mordor. They must go to Minis Ithil, the Tower of the Moon, built by the men of Gondor as a fortress against Sauron near the end of the Second Age. Within a hundred years, it was conquered by Sauron's forces, who held it less than a decade before Sauron's defeat. It then passed back into the hands of men, who held it for two millennia before the Nazgûl recaptured it. Now for over a thousand years, now called Minis Morgul, it has been under Sauron's control.

Sam argues that this is no better than where they are now, just another fortress under Sauron's thumb. But Gollum explains slyly, that while that is true, Sauron cannot see everywhere at once. He expects to be attacked at the Black Gate, not in Minis Morgul. When Gollum escaped from Mordor, he found a dark tunnel that led to a path across the mountain into Mordor. This time it is Frodo who presses him hard, for Aragorn told him that Gollum didn't escape, he was allowed to leave by Sauron in order to hunt for the Ring. Gollum protests indignantly that he did escape on his own. While it was true that he was told to seek the Precious, he searched, but for himself. "The precious was ours, it was mine. I tell you. I did escape."[132]

Frodo notices that in Gollum's self-defense, "our" and "we" gave way to "mine" and "I." In the past, when that happened, Gollum was at least partially truthful. But still, this is a dangerous undertaking, and one in which they would once more be led by an increasingly untrustworthy Gollum. But what other choice does he have. And so it is off to Minis Morgul that they go.

So now they follow a path that Gollum intends to lead to the death of Frodo and Sam, so that he can regain the Ring. But in his treachery, he shows them the only path that could ever have led them to complete the quest. There are many moral ambiguities we encounter once we decide to move through the darkness.

Not long on their journey, however, while Gollum is off hunting food, Frodo and Sam encounter Faramir and his warriors from Gondor. The story of that encounter belongs in the following chapters, for it shows all three of Frodo, Sam, and Faramir at their finest. While the three are sizing each other up and concluding they like what they see, Faramir's men spy Gollum fishing. When they ask if they should shoot him with their bows and arrows, Frodo begs for his life, and even reveals, to Faramir's astonishment, that Gollum once bore the Ring. So Gollum's life is spared, but Frodo is forced to deceive Gollum in order to capture him. Though it is only by doing so that Gollum is allowed to live, Gollum only sees that Master betrayed him to the nasty men. Eventually, they are all allowed to return to their quest.

GOLLUM'S BETRAYAL AND REDEMPTION

On they go, with Frodo now so tired that he notices little of their journey; even Sam struggles to keep up with Gollum's relentless pace. Three more days pass until finally Gollum leads them to the entrance to Shelob's Lair; Shelob—the "She" Sam heard Gollum mention in his moral debate with himself—is an enormous spider so ancient that she probably goes back to the First Age. Somehow in his earlier wanderings after leaving Mordor, Gollum has made a pact with Shelob, he brings her food—Orcs, now hobbits—and she allows him safe passage through her tunnel. While Frodo and Sam drop exhausted to the ground, Gollum goes off to tell Shelob he is bringing her more food. After Shelob is through with them, Gollum figures that he will gather up his Precious and become himself Master of the Ring.

But Gollum has one last moment of moral conflict. When he returns from Shelob, he finds Sam and Frodo lying asleep, Frodo's head in Sam's lap, Sam's hand on his brow. Something moves inside Gollum, some emotion he has not felt in many years. "Very cautiously he touched Frodo's knee—but almost the touch was a caress. For a fleeting moment, could one of the sleepers have seen him, they would have thought that they beheld an old weary hobbit, shrunken by the years that had carried him beyond his time, beyond friends and kin, and the fields and streams of youth, an old starved pitiable thing."[133]

One of the most touching scenes in The Lord of the Rings. For one brief moment, Gollum might have redeemed himself. But if he had, perhaps then he would not have fulfilled his destiny, the destiny tied so deeply to the fate of the Ring.

But that moment of peace, when Gollum might have become Sméagol once more and spared their lives from Shelob, was ruined when Sam awoke. Seeing Gollum leaning over Frodo, he thinks the worst and accuses him of sneaking off on some villain's errand, as of course he did. And at that, Sméagol reverts to Gollum for the last time, and continues on with his betrayal. He leads them into the tunnel that is Shelob's Lair. As they enter, the smell inside is so loathsome that they almost turn back. But if this is the only way forward, then forward through the tunnel they must go.

But we have to leave them there, lost in Shelob's Lair, for the story of all that happened with Sam and Frodo after they were left by Gollum to be Shelob's food, belongs to their chapters. Here we are concerned with Gollum, so we must move forward in time, to the very end of the Quest, at the top of Mount Doom. Frodo and Sam are standing on the lip of the volcano, the only fire that can destroy the Ring. They have come so far, suffered so much, for this moment. And then something unexpected happens. Frodo, too, is finally overpowered by the temptations of the Ring. At the point when he must fulfil his destiny and throw the Ring into the volcano, he finds that he can't. Like Isildur, who refused to destroy the Ring when he had a chance; like Gollum, who killed to get the Ring; like Bilbo, who was ready to attack Gandalf as a thief for suggesting he give up the Ring; Frodo, too, cannot part with it. He must have it for himself. He slips it on his finger and vanishes from sight.

And then, in his greed for his Precious, Gollum accomplishes the greatest deed of his life. He has been stalking Frodo and Sam. Just a few moments before, he tried to get the Ring from Frodo, but Frodo held it forth and commanded him to fall down before him. Prophetically, Frodo tells him "If you touch me ever again, you shall be cast into the Fire of Doom."[134] But now, just as Frodo puts on the Ring, Gollum jumps on Frodo, struggles with him, then bites off Frodo's ring finger and takes the Ring. He has one brief moment of satisfaction, dancing in his joy at finally being re-united with his Precious. Then, having come too close to the edge in his struggle, he pitches backward into the Volcano, clutching the Ring as he falls to his death. And thus, at the end of this long journey, it is evil Gollum who fulfils the Quest and destroys the Ring.

Before the Quest had properly begun, Gandalf speculated that Gollum would play some role in the Quest, whether for good or for evil, he did not know. And so Gollum did play a role, a central role, both for good and for evil. Without Gollum's aid as their guide, Frodo and Sam would never have made it into Mordor, to Mount Doom. Without his treachery, Frodo and Sam would not have come so close to death at the fangs of Shelob. Without Gollum's covetousness for his Precious, Frodo would have failed in his task and Sauron would have won the war. Gollum, flawed as he was, fulfilled his destiny; he played the role of villain in order that heroes might live.

Chapter Six
The Path of Love

In earlier chapters, we've already seen two inseparable pairs: Merry and Pippin, Legolas and Gimli. Merry and Pippin are like two peas in a pod, so alike that only their age differences separate them at all, with Pippin merely a younger version of Merry. Legolas and Gimli are total opposites who, when they first meet, are constantly at odds; later they come to respect their opposite and become inseparable friends. Frodo and Sam are still another inseparable pair, but joined in quite a different way than either Merry and Pippin, or Legolas and Gimli.

Unlike all the others in the Fellowship, Sam comes from a lower economic class. Upon Bilbo's unexpected departure, Frodo becomes the Master of the finest house in Hobbiton. But whether that had happened or not, Frodo had still been raised in the upper class of Hobbit society, along with his dear friends Merry and Pippin. In contrast, Sam was a simple gardener, borne into this lower strata of society as generations before him had been. Sam works as a gardener, first for Bilbo, then later for Frodo. Despite their obvious affection for each other, and their total dependence on each other as the quest continues, Sam and Frodo never step fully out of their class roles. It would be unthinkable for Sam to consider himself Frodo's equal.

At the time Tolkien wrote this book, England was still very nearly as stratified by class as it might have been in the Middle Ages (or Middle Earth). When he served in World War I, he was automatically an officer, along with every other member of his class, while those of Sam's class of society were automatically the enlisted men. Each officer had a "batman," a sort of butler who took care of the material details of his life. Many years later, talking of the war, Tolkien said that he preferred the enlisted men to the officers. "My 'Sam Gamgee' is indeed a reflexion of the English soldier, of the privates and batmen I knew in the 1914 war, and recognized as so far superior to myself."[135]

Throughout the book, Sam is unwavering in his love for, and devotion to, Frodo. Though such a rigid class structure may seem strange and even repugnant to us who have grown up in America, there is probably no better picture in literature of the possibility of love between two men, totally without any need to even consider homosexual attraction. Their separation by their class allows Sam to love Frodo unashamedly and Frodo to love Sam equally in turn. Though Sam, along with Pippin and sometimes Gollum, provides the necessary touches of humor to Tolkien's story, Sam is far more than a figure of fun. Though Frodo's affection for Sam is occasionally condescending, viewing him from the height of his educated upper class, Frodo never truly looks down on Sam. His jokes at Sam's expense come from both respect and deep affection.

A LOVE OF ELVES

Sam is as much a part of the earth as the trees and the flowers. Throughout the book Sam never wavers in his love for their home in the Shire. With his peasant suspicion of anything new and different, which contrasts so strikingly with Merry and Pippin's intense curiosity, there is one thing that does evoke Sam's curiosity: Elves! Our first encounter with Sam is in an argument he has with Ted Sandyman in The Green Dragon, where we find that Sam believes in the existence of Ents and loves Elves. Though he could never get enough of Bilbo's stories of his adventures, it was when they concerned Elves that his ears really pricked up. And we find throughout the story that Sam doesn't miss much.

Though rooted in the earth, Sam has a love of the magical, the exotic: of Ents and Oliphaunts and, especially, Elves. It is this touchstone inside him that gives his love of the earth a dignity that is lacking in his more hidebound fellow Hobbits. Because of this touch of magic, whenever Sam unexpectedly says something wise or poetic, we don't find it out of place.

We next meet Sam when Gandalf is telling Frodo about the Ring, and catches Sam snooping outside the window. Dragged inside by Gandalf, Sam is beside himself with fear that Gandalf might do something awful to him. But, after getting over his fear, he's delighted that he will be allowed to accompany Frodo and actually see some Elves. Still first things first: before they leave, Frodo finds Sam in the cellar of Frodo's house having one last long draught of the beer stored there.

Here, at the beginning, Sam is simply a funny character who we think will provide laughs. But as the Quest continues, he will become far more.

On the way to The Inn of the Prancing Pony, Sam and company actually meet Elves. In years to come, Sam remembers the evening spent with the Elves "as one of the chief events of his life." In trying to describe it, he praised the food, which the Elves described as "poor fare," saying "if I could grow apples like that, I would call myself a gardener." Then he added "But it was the singing that went to my heart, if you know what I mean."[136]

Our first glimpse of the poetry within Sam's soul. We couldn't imagine Merry or Pippin or even Frodo saying something both so simple and so profound.

The Elves sense Sam's quality, since, like Gandalf before them, they ask him never to leave Frodo. He reassures them that he would never do so. When Frodo asks Sam if, now that he's met the Elves, he still likes them, Sam says wisely "They seem a bit above my likes and dislikes, so to speak. It don't seem to matter what I think about them. They are quite different from what I expected—so old and young, and so gay and sad, as it were."[137] Sam continues, telling Frodo that meeting the Elves has changed things inside him and now he has a feeling what their journey is about. "I know we are going to take a very long road, into darkness….I have something to do before the end, and it lies ahead, not in the Shire."[138]

It is always Sam, rooted in the earth, who both sees the farthest, and looks the deepest.

CROSSING BOUNDARIES

Like most hobbits (and unlike the more adventurous Frodo, Merry and Pippin), Sam has never been on water. When the hobbits cross the Brandywine, he has his first doubts that he should have ever left the Shire. But not even water, of which he'll see much more in the days to come, will deter Sam from accompanying his master. And, despite his fears, during the crossing, Sam's sharp eyes spot a dark figure across the way, their first glimpse of Gollum.

At the *Inn of the Prancing Pony* in Bree, when Strider appears unexpectedly in their room, it is Sam who is immediately ready to spring to his master's defense, and Sam who continues to remain suspicious of Strider long after the others have accepted him. We see in this both Sam's peasant distrust of anyone out of the ordinary, and his intense protectiveness for Frodo. Clearly Sam would do anything to defend Frodo, as he has too often enough during their quest.

> *In such situations, we see both the strength of Sam's love and the limits of his peasant's perception. Frodo is able to see Strider's honesty and quality before Sam.*

After the company wakes to find their old rooms destroyed by the Black Riders, and all the ponies and horses in the town of Bree are gone, the only pony they are able to buy at any price is a sad-looking creature than no one else would want. But Sam takes charge of Bill (as he names the pony) and Bill responds to Sam's love and care. That, together with the special attention he later gets from the Elves in Rivendell, soon has Bill as healthy and hardy as a young colt. Sam's heart nearly breaks when later, outside the mines of Moria, they are forced to turn Bill loose. But wise Gandalf, who can speak to animals as he does to men and hobbits, tells Bill to find his way back safely to wherever he chooses to go. And, in fact, after the quest is over and the Hobbits stop at *The Inn of the Prancing Pony* on their way back to the Shire, Sam is overjoyed to find that

Bill is safe and sound. He takes him with him, never to be parted from him again

At the council in Rivendell, Elrond agrees that Frodo is the right person to be the Ring-bearer. When Sam jumps up and insists Frodo can't go alone, Elrond is pleased and says that Sam can accompany Frodo. But he can't resist teasing him a little, saying that he could hardly keep him from accompanying Frodo since he can't even keep Sam out of a secret council meeting. Sam blushes and says "A nice pickle we have landed ourselves in, Mr. Frodo!"[139]

Time and again throughout the story, Sam impulsively blurts out thoughts that wiser heads would keep to themselves. Each time though these outbursts lead to a good outcome. Though here, as on other occasions, Sam is a source of humor for the others, note that wise Elrond chooses him as the first of Frodo's companions.

ELVES AND ELVES

Sam has met the Elves along the road on their way to Rivendell, and met many more, including Elrond, in Rivendell. Then he meets still another group of Elves in Galadriel's forest kingdom of Lothlórien. While there, Frodo asks Sam what he now thinks of Elves. Sam, now wiser, says simply "I reckon there's Elves and Elves. They're all elvish enough, but they're not all the same."[140] In fact, he feels more kin to those of Lothlórien. Like the Hobbits of the Shire, these Elves are part and parcel of the land they live in. Though he still feels their power, however, he is a little disappointed that the magic he had expected is hidden deep in these Elves.

This is a very deep insight indeed, to be able to see a sameness between Hobbits like himself, rooted in the earth, and the airy, magical Elves. But it's nevertheless a true insight.

Soon afterwards though, Galadriel presents him with something very Elvish and magical, when she lets him look into the Mirror of Galadriel. When Sam looks into the water, hoping to see what is happening in his beloved Shire, he sees first Frodo lying asleep under a cliff. Then he sees the Shire, but a Shire where the trees have been cut down and smoke is belching from a red brick factory. He immediately wants to return home, but Galadriel explains that the Mirror doesn't necessarily show what is, or even what will be, but simply possibilities. No mater, this is still too much for Sam, who says "I wish I had never come here, and I don't want to see no more magic."[141] But even this isn't enough to dissuade Sam from his responsibility toward Frodo; he says that he'll continue on their quest.

> *There is nothing Sam could imagine that would hurt him more than a Shire in ruins, but his bravery will not allow him to stop. Note that he also sees a vision of Frodo lying seemingly dead after Shelob's sting, but it is too early to understand its meaning. When we experience visions, insights from within, often they have this complex quality: they might be showing what is, or what might be, or might even be a lie. And even if true, we may not yet know what they mean. But nevertheless, we should never overlook the opportunity to look into the Mirror of Galadriel.*

FRODO, SAM, & GOLLUM

After Boromir tries to steal the Ring, Frodo decides that the Ring is too much temptation for any one else to bear. He decides that he must continue on the quest alone. He goes down to the river and pushes off in one of the Elven boats. But he underestimates the extent of Sam's devotion. When Sam sees Frodo sailing away, he immediately jumps in the water to follow him, forgetting in his haste that he doesn't know how to swim. Crying out "coming, Mr. Frodo! Coming!"[142] Sam immediately sinks like a stone. But Frodo hears his cries, brings the boat back and pulls him up to safety. Frodo tries to dissuade him, reminding him that the journey is to Mordor, but Sam is determined to stick with Frodo no matter what comes their way. Though Frodo didn't wish his destiny on any of his friends, he is so happy to have Sam with him, that he laughs out loud in joy. And then they continue on their journey, alone except for each other.

> *From here on, the pair is inseparable. Even when the Ring drives Frodo to suspicion of everyone, including Sam, Sam never once wavers in his love for, and*

loyalty to, Frodo. We all need to experience both roles in our life: unwavering love for another, and having someone love us that deeply.

Frodo is indeed lucky to have such a companion. Sam, ever the practical one, takes care of their physical needs. He carries everything that can be carried, knowing that Frodo is weighted down enough by the drag of the Ring. Sam takes charge of what little provisions there are, cooking when that is still possible, then later apportioning the meager stock of water and Elven waybread. He is the one who was wise enough to bring along a length of Elven rope, without which they could never have made their way through otherwise impassable mountainous areas. When Gollum finds them rabbits, it's Sam who cooks them. No matter how dark their situation, and how gloomy Frodo's mood, Sam is always able to find something to be happy about. A very fine companion indeed!

It is because of Sam's rootedness in earthy reality that he is always practical, always thinking of the necessities of life. We all need a Sam to balance our Frodo.

Three days after leaving the others, Frodo and Sam are totally lost, with no idea how to get to Mordor. In exasperation, Sam exclaims: "What a fix! That's the one place in all the lands we've ever heard of that we don't want to see any closer; and that's the one place we're trying to get to! And that's just where we can't get nohow."[143] They desperately need a guide; that guide soon appears in the unlikely person of Gollum. If Sam was originally wary of Gandalf and suspicious of Strider, his distrust of Gollum is much deeper. Though Sam acquiesces to Frodo's decision to take Gollum/Smeagol as a guide, nothing Frodo says will ever change his opinion of Gollum. Sam is only able to see part of the picture; unlike Frodo, Sam is unable to look deeper into Smeagol and see the possibility of redemption. Sam knows a villain when he sees him, and Frodo is lucky that Sam is along to keep a careful eye on Smeagol.

Much of the story is in this dynamic among the three, with Sam unwavering in his devotion to Frodo and his quest, and unbending in his animosity toward Gollum. As we saw in the previous chapter on Gollum, from the point when Gollum joins them and becomes their guide, Sam, Frodo and Gollum are tied together in a tight knot, with

Gollum/Smeagol pulled toward his best side by Frodo's kindness and trust, toward his worst side by Sam's insults and distrust. Frodo is also pushed and pulled by the dynamic. As they grow ever closer to Mordor, the Ring grows more powerful and perhaps Frodo would have yielded to it sooner except for his compassion toward Gollum, and the protection of Sam. And even Sam, ever optimistic, might have despaired if he wasn't so busy protecting Frodo from Gollum. The dynamic is the most complex of any in *The Lord of the Rings*.

It must be said that his dislike of Gollum gives Sam energy and sometimes even pleasure. As we pointed out in the previous chapter, the lembas tasted especially good to Sam after he found that Gollum despised them. Gollum in turn laughs out loud when Sam trips and falls face first into the dead marshes and sees the dead faces staring up at him. Neither of the two sees anything to like in the other; they are only joined because of their joint allegiance to Frodo.

Sam's continued distrust of Gollum serves them well for it is he who first notices a subtle change in Smeagol after they are all frightened by Black Riders flying overhead. And then when he overhears the schizophrenic dialogue between Gollum's two sides, Sam is canny enough not to confront Gollum, and not to weigh Frodo down with still another problem. But he knows now definitely that Frodo is wrong and Gollum is plotting something evil. If only he knew who "She" was.

So in this three-way dynamic, we see the strengths and weaknesses of all three characters. Sam is too simple to ever see the good buried deep inside Gollum. But he is also too shrewd to ever be fooled when Gollum pretends to a friendliness that is only skin-deep.

CONFRONTING FARAMIR

A little later, while Gollum is off hunting for food, Frodo and Sam are confronted by Faramir and his men. Frodo and Faramir both speak cautiously, both reluctant to show their full hand until they know with whom they are dealing. When Faramir asks about the third member of their party, Frodo deflects the question, saying that he is only someone they met by chance on their journey. Then he tells who they are and of the company they started out with. At the mention of Boromir, Faramir and company are startled and now want to know much more.

Frodo again proceeds cagily, asking if Faramir knows the "riddling words"[144] that led Boromir to Rivendell. Faramir does indeed, having been the first to have the dream that brought Boromir to Rivendell. But he does not reveal this to Frodo, merely saying that he does know the "riddling words." Frodo is then willing to reveal that they are the Halflings of the riddle, and that the Sword that was Broken belongs to Aragorn. But he's not willing to discuss Isildur's Bane. In this and future exchanges between the two, regardless of their mutual suspicion, both Faramir and Frodo are impeccably courteous, a marked contrast to Faramir's brother Boromir.

While the hobbits are detained, ostensibly as guests, a battle arises between Faramir's men and men from the South—Haradrim—who are in alliance with Sauron. Hobbits are peaceful folk, fond of the good things in life, with little taste for war, so Sam watches the battle with horror. But then one thing does fascinate him: the sight of Mûmak—a mammoth far bigger than the elephants of our own day. Sam exclaims: "An Oliphaunt it was! . . . So there are Oliphaunts, and I have seen one."[145]

Sam gets to see another of the wonders he had so desired to see. Note how much he has to sacrifice along the journey in order to experience these wonders. Often people go too lightly into the exotic realms inside them, looking only for magic, not realizing that they must also experience pain and loss.

With the battle concluded, Faramir returns to his questioning of Frodo, trying to force Frodo to disclose what Isildur's Bane is and where it is hidden. Frodo tells him only that it belongs to no mortal; but if it did, it would probably be Aragorn. When Faramir wonders why Aragorn, Frodo reveals that Aragorn is the heir of Isildur. This arouses excitement in the company, and more suspicion in Faramir, who knows Boromir is dead and wants to know to what degree Frodo and the others, including Aragorn, were involved in his death. When Frodo tells him that he is not at liberty to discuss his mission, and that Faramir should not interfere with it, Faramir grows angry and answers "So! You bid me mind my own affairs, and get me back home, and let you be. Boromir will tell all, when he comes, say you! Were you a friend of Boromir?"[146] And Frodo is forced to answer cautiously that "I was a friend, for my part."[147]

At that, Faramir lays some of his cards on the table, with the revelation that Boromir is dead. Frodo is appalled, both by the unexpected bad news, but also by Faramir trying to trap him in lies. When Faramir accuses Frodo of treachery, Sam has had enough of this haughty man who is insulting his master. Just as he jumped up at the Council of Elrond, he interjects himself into the conversation now, saying "Begging your pardon, Mr. Frodo, but this has gone on long enough. He has no right to talk to you so. After all you've gone through, as much for his good and all these great Men as for anyone else."[148] He stands in front of Faramir and dresses him down in no uncertain terms, just as if he was talking to an insolent young hobbit. The sight of this little fellow so quick to defend his master defuses the situation as nothing else could have done.

As so many times in the story, Sam blurts out his honest feelings. Each time, this provokes laughter, but also each time the listeners recognize the truth in what he has to say.

Many of the men grin at the sight, and when Faramir answers, his anger is gone and he is now willing to reveal all. He tells them that he has been commanded to kill anyone they find loose in the land. And thus he has every right to confront Frodo with suspicion. After telling Sam to sit down and be quiet—which he does—he finally reveals that Boromir is his brother. When he then asks Frodo if he can remember anything special about Boromir's gear that would prove he knew him, Frodo decides to trust his instinct that Faramir is a better, wiser man than his brother. He tells him that Boromir carried a horn.

This is enough to convince Faramir that they indeed knew Boromir. He tells them that eleven days earlier, he heard that horn at the edge of his mind, as if it might have been a dream. Then that night he had a vision of a dead Boromir floating by in the boat. His body is covered with wounds and he has a broken sword on his knee. And a golden belt which Faramir does not recognize. But no horn! The pieces of the horn later drifted to shore by themselves. Frodo sadly tells him that the boat in which he lay, and the belt he wore, were both given by Galadriel, but that he can say no more, as Boromir was alive when last he saw him.

Though much is still left unsaid still between Faramir and Frodo, the crisis has passed. They are all willing to open up more, though Frodo still keeps Boromir's treachery and the identity of Isildur's Bane to himself. Unlike Frodo, Sam's mouth sometimes gets the better of him. When talking of Boromir, Sam speaks out of turn, and reveals that "From the moment he first saw it he wanted the Enemy's Ring."[149]

This is most dangerous of all Sam's gaffes. But somehow, deep inside, Sam must have known that Faramir could be trusted.

Faramir smiles and says softly that he now understands everything: Frodo is carrying the One Ring, Boromir tried to steal it, and they escaped. Now they have fallen into Faramir's hands. "A pretty stroke of fortune! A chance for Faramir, Captain of Gondor, to show his quality!"[150] Both Frodo and Sam jump up, pulling out their little swords, as if they were a match for this warrior, even if he didn't have his men about him. But Faramir is simply playing with them. He laughs and says that he is wise enough (as were Gandalf and Aragorn and Galadriel) not to desire the Ring for himself. Like Aragorn, he tells them that he will do anything within his power to help them in their quest.

Later Sam finds an opportunity to approach Faramir. He bows low, then tells him: "[You] showed your quality, the very highest."[151] When Faramir insists that no praise is deserved, Sam adds: "you said my master had an elvish air; and that was good and true. But I say this: you have an air, too, sir, that reminds me of, of—well, Gandalf, of wizards."[152] And so Faramir does, having been wise enough to study at Gandalf's feet, despite the contempt his father Denethor and brother Boromir felt for such knowledge.

Just as Sam doesn't mind dressing down Faramir as if he was a naughty child, Sam also doesn't worry about the audacity of a servant praising a mighty lord. As always, he sees deep and true.

THE BATTLE WITH SHELOB

After Faramir releases Gollum to Frodo and Sam, the three continue on their way. Smeagol has lost his inner struggle with his Gollum personality and now plans to lead the hobbits into the caverns of the giant spider Shelob. While resting at the entrance to the caves, Sam delivers one of the most beautiful speeches in *The Lord of the Rings*.

The brave things in the old tales and songs, Mr. Frodo: adventures, as I used to call them. I used to think that they were things the wonderful folk of the stories went out and looked for, because they wanted them, because they were exciting and life was a bit dull, a kind of sport, as you might say. But that's not the way of it with the tales that really mattered, or the ones that stay in your mind. Folk seem to have been just landed in them, usually—their paths were laid that way, as you put it. But I expect they had lots of chances, like us, of turning back, only they didn't. And if they had, we shouldn't know, because they'd have been forgotten. We hear about those as just went on.[153]

Is there any better summary possible of what makes this quest important? Could any other character have expressed it better?

Perhaps even Frodo would have turned back and his tale been forgotten if he hadn't had the ever loyal Sam along to support him every step of the way. From here on in their joint quest, Frodo is to need Sam's friendship and support even more than he already has.

Once inside the cave, the stench is unlike anything they have ever smelled before. But Gollum insists that this is the only way to get into Mordor. He leads them deep into the caverns then silently steals away. On their own, fearing that Gollum has betrayed them, Frodo and Sam stumble forward. Then, from behind they hear sounds, terrible sounds; when they turn to see what is following them, they can see nothing in the gloomy darkness. As so often before, Sam comes to the rescue: he remembers the star-glass that Galadriel gave to Frodo, a phial that contains a light that will shine when all other lights fail. When Frodo pulls it out of his tunic, it begins to burn, then shines brighter and brighter, as if it were a miniature star.

In the light, they now see the giant she-spider Shelob advancing on them. Frodo and Sam back away, then lose their courage and run. As Shelob gains ground, Frodo realizes that running is useless. In an act of incredible bravery, he turns, pulls out Sting, raises the star-glass before him, and advances on Shelob. For many thousands of years, Shelob has lived inside her cavern, protected from the light of the sun, and now she is faced by a light brighter than anything in her long memory. It is Shelob who retreats from the little hobbit, slinking into one of her many passages. Sam cries out to Frodo that the Elves will make a song of his heroism. But as this is no time to stop and talk of such things, Sam grabs Frodo and pulls him on, in a rush to get out of the cavern before Shelob returns.

When they come to the tunnel's exit, they find it covered by a spider web, each strand as thick as a rope. Sam laughs at the "cobwebs" and begins to hack at them with his sword; but the strands are stronger than his sword. Frodo hands Sam the star-glass while he tries Sting on the web. Forged by Elves, Sting cuts through the strands of web like a hot knife through butter. Frodo runs through the opening, out from the cave, yelling for Sam to follow. But Shelob has never allowed prey to escape before and doesn't intend to let this prey escape either.

Out in the open, Sam sees that Sting is glowing with a blue flame, which means that Orcs are about. Quickly, he hides the star-glass inside a pocket so that the Orcs will not be attracted by the light. The light is barely hidden when Sam sees Shelob emerge from one of her many hidden exits, directly behind Frodo. When Sam tries to cry out a warning, Gollum jumps on his back, with his hand covering Sam's mouth. This is one of Gollum's favorite tricks, a way he has killed many creatures: grab from behind, wrap his arms and legs around his victim, then crush the life out of them. As Gollum squeezes harder, Sam's sword falls to the ground. Sam tries one last desperate maneuver: he plants his feet firmly, then flings himself backwards against the ground with all of his might. When Gollum hits the ground with Sam's full weight crushing his chest, he momentarily loosens his grip. Sam breaks free and begins to beat Gollum with his staff. When Sam picks up his sword to finish him off, Gollum scuttles away on all fours back into the tunnel.

Freed from Gollum's grasp, Sam runs after Shelob, only to find Frodo already wrapped in a cocoon of Shelob's web, with Shelob dragging the body away to serve as a future meal. Without even a pause to consider his own safety, Sam springs at Shelob and begins to hack away with his sword. So furious is his attack, and so surprised is Shelob, that Sam manages first to cut off a claw, then to stab one of her many eyes. He rushes underneath her belly, then tries to cut her belly. But Shelob is too tough to be killed by Sam's sword; she simply drops straight down onto Sam, intending to crush him with her enormous body, as she has crushed others before him. But Sam drops his own sword, picks up Sting, and holds it point upwards. Shelob's weight drives the Elven blade deep into her belly. Shelob has never known such agony and shrieks in pain. Instinctively, she springs away, then turns to sting Sam, as she has already stung Frodo. But Sam pulls out the Phial of Galadriel, and with Elven words he has never spoken before coming unbidden to his tongue, he advances on Shelob as his master had before. Tormented by the pain of her wounds, confronted once again by this dread light, Shelob gives up the fight and crawls slowly back into her lair.

Sam is here indeed a mighty warrior, the only one in history to vanquish Shelob. He is able to accomplish this great feat because he is totally selfless—he acts unconsciously in defense of Frodo, much like a mother who is able to lift an automobile off her child.

Sam turns then to Frodo and uses Sting to cut him free from the cocoon. But it's seemingly too late; Frodo appears dead. Sam can find no pulse, not the slightest breath of air. Crying out to Frodo, pleading with him to wake, Sam rubs Frodo's hands and feet, trying to generate some life, but he is cold as death. Sam remembers the vision of Frodo he saw in Galadriel's Mirror, lying pale and unmoving as he is now. But he knows now that Frodo wasn't sleeping in the vision, he was dead! All is lost. What can he do?

MASTER SAMWISE THE RING-BEARER

Sam has gone through too much in too short a time. Overwhelmed with grief and despair, he simply loses consciousness for a spell. When he wakes, he finds himself still on the ground beside his dead master. With Frodo dead, he feels that the whole quest has been for naught. But then he remembers his own words to Frodo after meeting his first set of Elves, back when their quest had hardly begun: "I have something to do before the end, and it lies ahead, not in the Shire."[154] He knows that now it is he who must continue the quest—alone.

He does what little he can for Frodo. He lays him on his back with his hands folded against his chest, as if asleep. He places his own sword and staff with him, and wraps his cloak around him. He can't leave Sting or Galadriel's star-glass, but Frodo is still wearing the mithril vest given him by Bilbo, which is worth a king's ransom (and which will indirectly lead to his rescue). Having done all he can do, he tries to leave, somehow he can't. Instead he stays kneeling by Frodo, holding his hand, struggling within himself.

How can he accomplish something that his master wasn't able to do? He is a simple gardener who only came along as Frodo's servant. It wasn't he who was given the Ring of Power by the council of Elrond. Who is he to take the Ring and continue on, as if Frodo had never existed? But Elrond, wise Elrond, didn't let Frodo go alone; he appointed companions to help Frodo accomplish his task. Since Sam is now the last of the fellowship of the Ring, if Middle-Earth is to survive, it is left to him to complete the quest.

Sam gently takes the Ring from around Frodo's neck. When even that doesn't make Frodo stir, Sam knows at last that Frodo must be dead; only death could free him of the responsibility for carrying the Ring. Begging Frodo's forgiveness, he puts the chain holding on the Ring around his own neck. He nearly falls to the ground when, for the first time, he experiences its terrible weight. Then he moves off into the dark.

Perhaps the bravest thing Sam ever does, even though he is wrong in assuming that Frodo is dead. Sam is stepping beyond the limits of his class, of what someone like him is capable of being. Yet, with no other alternative, he doesn't shrink from the obligations to serve a force greater than himself.

He has hardly started when he hears Orcs both in front and behind him. He's trapped. What to do? Like Bilbo and Frodo before him in similar binds, he pulls off the chain and slips the Ring onto his finger. And vanishes before the Orcs can see him! In the twilight world of the Ring, he discovers he possesses another power: the ability to understand the speech of the Orcs, perhaps because they are Sauron's servants and the Ring links all who belong to Sauron. Several of the Orcs spot Frodo and pick up the body. At the thought of Frodo's body desecrated by Orcs, Sam's resolve to continue the quest on his own fades away. He can't leave Mr. Frodo!

When the Orcs carry Frodo's body back into Shelob's lair, one remarks that they should be safe from Her tonight. Sam can do nothing but follow. Once they arrive at a central gathering place, Sam listens to their talk and learns much. The Orcs had been warned by the Nazgûl to watch for spies. Warned, they spotted Gollum, who they identified as Shelob's sneak. Evidently she leaves him alone because he himself is not worth eating and, in exchange for his life, he brings her food. One of the smarter Orcs is afraid of who else might be out there. After all someone had to cut Frodo's cords and someone had to stab Shelob. That thought frightens the others, as no one has ever before stood up to Shelob. They decide it must be a great Elf Warrior armed with both sword and axe.

And then Sam hears something that shakes him: the hobbit they found must be taken to the tower as a prisoner. He's not dead, only paralyzed by Shelob's sting! Sam immediately berates himself for not trusting his heart, which told him to stay with Frodo no matter what. "Don't trust your head, Samwise, it is not the best part of you."[155]

And we know this is true: Sam is a feeler, not a thinker. He acts instinctively, for better or worse.

Frodo is carried away to the watch tower at Cirith Ungol, the tower that is used as much to prevent escape from within Sauron's domain as to discourage attacks from without. Sam is determined to somehow save Frodo, but he knows it won't be easy to slip into the very lair of their enemies and bring out Frodo. But somehow he does just that. He knows that he must not use the Ring this close to Sauron, so he keeps it around his neck as he slips into the tower. He slowly makes his way up toward the top, where he suspects Frodo must be held.

As he goes, he passes hundreds of dead Orcs. When Frodo was stripped of his clothing and possessions, the Orcs discovered the mithril coat of mail given him by Bilbo. Of almost unimaginable worth, it is enough to split the uneasy alliance of the leaders of two factions of Orcs, both of whom covet the mithril vest. Orcs need little excuse to fight and their greed clears the way for Sam to make his way safely to Frodo. Several times individual Orcs spot him, but their fear of the supposed Elf warrior who could beat off Shelob leads them to see Sam as much more than he is, and to run away. Finally Sam comes to the very top of the tower and there is no Frodo. He fears that Frodo is already dead or carried away.

Then comes a key moment that so defines Sam. Sitting there, not knowing what to do, he begins to sing. And the song that comes out is composed on the spot, filled with both darkness and hope. It's a song that one would expect from a poet, not a simple gardener. But Sam has come a long way; he's hardly a simply gardener any more. Frodo, nearly unconscious, hears the song and tries to sing back. This upsets the Orc who has been left to guard him. He brings a ladder over, releases a trap-door, and goes up to beat Frodo with a whip. Sam is instantly up the ladder to defend Frodo. A slash of Sting and the Orc's whip-hand sails across the room. The Orc falls down the trap-door to his death. Frodo and Sam are reunited. All because of a song.

Again we see how far Sam has come. Poetry was for Elves or perhaps Mr. Bilbo, not for such as Sam. But he has come so far that now he is a poet as well as everything else. And his song saves Frodo.

Now, in between leaving Frodo behind as dead, then rescuing him, Sam has had his own crisis of faith with the Ring. Like all who wear it, even briefly, he has visions of himself as a mighty warrior, then almost as a gardener-god, with his own garden of Eden. But two things keep this from being much of a conflict for Sam: his love of Frodo, and his common-sense. He knows that the Ring is too great a thing for him to bear, and that these grandiose visions are only illusions. But remember that very few have been wise enough to know their limitations: Gandalf, Aragorn, Galadriel, Faramir—and Sam! He's in fine company. His words of praise for Faramir would apply equally to himself: "[You] showed your quality, the very highest."[156]

COMPLETION OF THE QUEST AND LIFE AFTERWARDS

Reunited with Frodo, Sam restores the Ring to its proper bearer, and the two begin the last leg of their long journey. Remember that Sam gives the Ring back willingly to Frodo. No one except Sam ever wears the Ring and willingly gives it over to another. Now inside Mordor itself, they move toward Orodruin—Mount Doom—the volcano in which the Ring was forged, and where they hope to destroy it. And this is more properly Frodo's story. But before we finish with Sam, we need to add a few details of what follows that speak to Sam's character.

Once more on their journey, Sam returns to his role as protector and provider for Frodo. There is little food left, just scraps of lembas, and less water. From here on, Sam gives Frodo nearly all the food and water, starving himself. Only Frodo is important to Sam now; his own welfare is immaterial. We see the limits of this in one of the most touching scenes in literature. So bowed down by the weight of the Ring that he is no longer able to even crawl, Frodo collapses at the foot of Mount Doom. Sam would readily bear the weight of the Ring if Frodo would let him, but he knows that he won't—the Ring is Frodo's burden to carry.

Each of us in some way comes to a point in our lives, where we realize that no one else can bear our burden, no matter how much they love us. This is the loneliest place on our journey, but also in some way the beginning of the last stage of the journey.[157]

But there is one more solution: if Sam can't carry the Ring for Frodo, he can carry Frodo! And so he does, lifting Frodo onto his back. Though the Ring is almost unimaginably heavy for its bearer, Sam finds the wasted away Frodo as light as a child. And so they continue up the slope of Mount Doom, where Frodo and Gollum combine to complete the Quest.

This marks the point where we know that only we can carry our burden, yet we no longer have the strength to do it alone. At that point, we find that if we are willing to give up our last vestiges of pride, there are loved ones who can carry us, even as we carry our burden. Even when there is no actual person around us to serve that function, we will find within us a force, humble and probably taken for granted, that can support us during these most difficult of all times.[158]

But there is life after the Quest, and no one's life is happier than Sam's. When the company left Lothlórien, Galadriel gave Sam a small, plain wooden box that contained earth from her personal orchard, earth that she had blessed. She told Sam that if he did manage to get home safely, he should sprinkle this earth on his garden. When Frodo's quest is completed and the Hobbits return to the Shire, they find it devastated, much like the picture Sam saw in the Mirror of Galadriel. As we discussed in the Path of Curiosity, Saruman, in his identity as Sharkey, has laid waste to the natural beauty of the Shire. But Sam is a gardener and gardeners plant. In the areas hit worst by Sharkey's destruction, Sam plants new young trees, placing a single grain of Galadriel's earth with each sapling. After completing his planting, he takes the little of Galadriel's precious earth which remains, goes to the Three-Farthing Stone, near the center of the Shire, and throws the dust into the air.

The next Spring is the most glorious in the history of the Shire. The weather is perfect, but even that isn't enough to explain how wonderfully fecund the growth. Not only do the new plants and trees and fruits and flowers flourish, even the children born that year are especially lovely and healthy. Many have Galadriel's golden hair. And the pipe-weed that the Hobbits love so well, and the ale brewed from the Barley, are both such as Hobbits remember with fondness for generations to come.

A year to the day after Aragorn's crowning as King Elessar, Sam marries his sweetheart: Rose Cotton. They live a long wonderful life together and have thirteen much loved children. When Frodo leaves Middle-Earth and sails over the Sea, he leaves Bag End to Sam. Once merely a servant, Sam is now master of the Shire's finest home. He goes on to become mayor of the Shire and serves seven terms of seven years each. When, in Sam's 102nd year, his beloved Rosie dies, he leaves Bag End and, according to legend, becomes the last of the Ring-bearers to pass over the Sea to the Blessed Realm.

Chapter Seven
The Path of Transcendence

We finally arrive at the most important character in *The Lord of the Rings*: Frodo the Ringbearer. Frodo's path transcends that of any other hero in literature. On the surface, the least likely of heroes, always aware of how ill-equipped he is to carry such a great burden, he accomplishes more than any of the seemingly greater figures like Kings and Wizards, Elves and Dwarves. The least becomes the greatest. Unlike all the other heros in the book, Frodo's task continues after the destruction of the Ring and the end of Sauron, even after the crowning of Aragorn as king, even after the battle for the Shire. The others move on with their lives, the darkness forgotten. But, Frodo, by carrying the weight of evil when no one else could or would, has looked too deeply into the darkness to ever again live fully in the light. Somehow he must find a way to live with that inner darkness, to integrate it into his life. That burden is now a part of his very being, something that he will have to struggle with to the end of his days. His is the modern condition that faces so many of us in our own path toward enlightenment and, hopefully, transcendence.

HOW BINGO BECAME FRODO

Tolkien had such a great success with his children's book, *The Hobbit*, that his publisher, Stanley Unwin, encouraged him to write a sequel. He initially tried to give Unwin some miscellaneous short stories for children, hoping that would satisfy him, but Unwin wanted Hobbits. Tolkien then passed on a voluminous pile of manuscript. This was his work on *The Silmarillion*, his long dreamed-of, and never-to-be-completed history of the First and Second Ages of the world (and what took place in the Third Age up to the days when the yet undreamt-of War of the Ring would take place). Unwin's in-house readers had no idea what to make of all this, and Unwin again pushed Tolkien to write something new about Hobbits. Eventually Tolkien gave way and began the story of Bilbo's birthday party. At this point, Tolkien knew nothing about the central significance the Ring was to later have in his story. Bilbo's vanishing was simply intended to be a prelude to further adventures where he went looking for still more dragon's gold.

As Tolkien wrote more, however, he soon realized that he had already said most of what he had to say about Bilbo. He decided to have Bilbo pass the Ring on to his son after the birthday party, and the son would become the hero of the new book. Since, at this point, he was still intending to write a tale for children, this character was called Bingo (!). Over time, however, as the story grew in darkness and the earlier parts were modified many times, Tolkien came to realize that this was no longer a children's story. The name Bingo seemed clearly inappropriate for this darker story, so Bingo disappeared and a previous minor character, Frodo, took his place. Happily for us.

In the final version that we read, Frodo is no longer Bilbo's son, but his much younger, favorite cousin. Typical of the way that Hobbits say something light when they mean something deep, before Bilbo's 99th birthday, he told Frodo (who was about to turn 21) that they might as well live together since they shared the same birthday (Sept. 22nd); that way they could share their birthday parties. And so from then on, Frodo lived with Bilbo. *The Lord of the Rings* opens twelve years later with the preparations for Bilbo's eleventy-first birthday, which will coincide with Frodo's 33rd birthday. Though, as we pointed out in chapter One, Hobbits are longer-lived than humans, still 111 is quite an age. And 33 marks the coming-of-age for Hobbits, so this is a propitious event for both Bilbo and Frodo.

At this point in the story, Frodo is presented as an amiable young (by Hobbit standards) Hobbit who clearly loves Bilbo. Only at the end of the chapter, after Bilbo has left the Shire, do we have the first inkling of the dangers that lie ahead for Frodo. Gandalf warns him to be careful of the Ring, whose full significance even Gandalf does not yet know. Bilbo has already told both of them separately the true story of how he acquired the Ring from Gollum, so that much they know. But they don't know yet that this is the Ring that belonged to Sauron, the One Ring that has power over all the other great Rings. Gandalf, however, already senses something and warns Frodo twice to be careful of the Ring and never use it: "keep it safe, and keep it secret."[159]

After Bilbo's departure, Frodo has seventeen years to enjoy himself as lord of the manor before Gandalf returns to start him on his Quest. When he reappears, Gandalf explains how dire the circumstances are already, with the nine Ring-Wraiths on their way to the Shire to find the Ring. Well-fed and happily indolent, Frodo hardly seems a likely candidate to accomplish great things. Yet Frodo immediately grasps how important it is to prevent Sauron from reacquiring the Ring. With no hesitation, he prepares to leave his comfortable home, not even knowing where he will go. Amazed by this display of bravery, Gandalf tells him that: "Hobbits really are amazing creatures ... You can learn all that there is to know about their ways in a month, and yet after a hundred years they can still surprise you at a pinch."[160]

And so are all of us "amazing creatures." When the necessity arises, if we turn away from all the things we think are important (like security and comfort) and instead look within, we can tap resources that we never knew we possessed, resources that go beyond our existence as mortal creatures. And each of us must at some time start the journey to fulfil our destiny, just as Frodo starts his journey.

Soon Frodo and his Hobbit companions (Merry, Pippin, and Sam) are on the road where their adventures start. After an encounter with a Black Rider, they meet a party of High Elves, led by Gildor. When Gildor offers them lodging for the night, Frodo surprises us with his scholarship, thanking Gildor gracefully in High Elven speech. Later in the night, he tells Gildor of his perilous situation and asks him for advice. When Gildor is overly subtle, seemingly reluctant to tell him anything, Frodo teases him: "Go not to the Elves for counsel, for they will say both no and yes."[161]

Often, when we turn to "experts" for advice, they do little but confuse us, presenting arguments for any option we could pick. The last thing they want to do is to take a moral stand, which might turn out to have bad consequences. So ultimately, we are forced back on our own judgement.

TOM BOMBADIL

In the Second Age of the world there were many great forests, but they were cut down by the Númenóreans, the great Men of the earlier Age from whom Aragorn descended. Now only two such great forests remain: the old Forest of the North, in which Frodo and his friends are wandering, and Fangorn in the South, which takes its name from Fangorn (Treebeard). Both forests remember how their fellow trees were destroyed by men, and neither is a welcome place for humans (or Hobbits) to visit. Frodo, however, hoping to avoid the Black Riders, decides to get off the road and take a "short cut" through the Old Forest of the North on their way to the Inn of the Prancing Pony. This short cut will turn out to be anything but short cut and will lead the Hobbits twice into danger, both times to be saved by Tom Bombadil. And it is Tom Bombadil that we need to understand because he alone stands outside all the troubles and strife of Middle Earth.

Once inside the Old Forest, the Hobbits are soon lost. After wandering to no purpose four hours, in a scene reminiscent of Dorothy and her companions on the field of poppies in "The Wizard of Oz, Frodo and his friends find themselves getting sleepier and sleepier. Merry and Pippin nap against a huge tree, the Old Willow Tree, while Frodo goes around to the river side of the tree, hoping to revive himself by bathing his face. Instead he, too, falls asleep, leaning against the tree. He wakens in distress to find that he's been thrown into the river by the Tree, whose roots are pushing him down beneath the water. Thankfully ever-faithful Sam hears Frodo's call for help and pulls him out before he drowns. When they look for Merry and Pippin, they find that Pippin has already been sucked inside the great tree, though a crack which has now closed up again. Merry has not yet been fully swallowed and is stuck half in and half out of the tree. All Frodo and Sam can think to do is to light a fire, hoping it will frighten the tree into releasing Merry and Pippin.

Instead it merely angers the Old Willow, which begins to squeeze Merry harder. With no idea what to do next, Frodo runs around calling for help.

Once we start our journey, which is always an inner journey, we are likely to encounter ancient, inhuman forces, forces that are never exposed to the light of day, the light of consciousness. They are rooted in the forces of nature themselves, and while not inherently evil, they are not fond of being disturbed. We do well to tread lightly in such circumstances.

Tom Bombadil appears, seemingly in answer to Frodo's call for help, singing a happy song, a song about himself and his lovely wife Goldberry. When he sees Merry and Pippin's predicament, he puts his mouth to the crack in the tree and sings into it, a song that tells the Old Willow to release the Hobbits. Then he breaks off a branch and begins to whack the tree with it, calling out "You let them out again, Old Man Willow! What be you a thinking of? You should not be waking. Eat earth! Dig Deep! Drink water! Go to sleep! Bombadil is talking!"[162]

If in danger against these ancient forces, often our only recourse is to appeal to higher power for help. Deep within us, we have access to such benevolent powers; the powers are not ours, but we can appeal to them through techniques such as Active Imagination.[163] When we do so, these powers will almost invariably take personified form— when we are dealing with forces beyond human definition, we humans seem to need to personify them in order to have a frame of reference we can accept. For example, when Jacob needed to struggle with divinity in order to bring forth a new self-definition, he experienced it as wrestling with a mysterious stranger. Bombadil is such a force, and as such beyond even something as old as the Willow. He reminds the Old Willow that it has its own life to live and should not be interfering in human lives, any more than they should be interfering in its life.

After rescuing the Hobbits, Tom takes them home with him to recover from their ordeal. Later that evening, while sitting with Bombadil and Goldberry over a wonderful dinner, Frodo asks whether Tom heard his call for help, or whether it was just a lucky chance that he appeared then. Tom says "just chance brought me then, if chance you call it. It was no plan of mine, though I was waiting for you."[164]

Time and time again once we are on our chosen path, we will find that synchronicities multiply. Chance becomes something other than chance when it has meaning and answers need. But not in a causal way that we are familiar with from our normal outer life. Rather fate is already waiting for us, even though we did not now we would take this particular path. Once we grow more used to such synchronicities, we see them everywhere in life. But in special times, including emergencies, synchronicities tend to multiply.

After spending a magical night with Tom Bombadil and Goldberry, and after a hearty breakfast (which no Hobbit would willingly miss) the next morning, the Hobbits hear Goldberry outside in the hills singing a song of rain. Soon everywhere around the house the rain pours down. Tom comes into the house, telling them that it's "Goldberry's washing day;"[165] Evidently, when a force of nature such as Goldberry washes, it's all of nature that she washes. With the rain pouring down, Tom sits down, gets comfortable, and begins to tell the Hobbits "tales of bees and flowers, the ways of trees, and the strange creatures of the Forest, about evil things and good things, things friendly and things unfriendly, cruel things and kind things, and secrets hidden under brambles."[166] And then he tells tales of men and their silly doings, of wars and pillaging, of kingdoms that rose and fell. And how now the spoils of those wars lie with the dead in barrows where ghosts, barrow-wights, sometimes walk.

Here we might have the best advice Tolkien can give us about the struggle with darkness that occupies the rest of the book, the struggle that leaves Frodo wounded for the rest of his life. Once we were a part of Nature, like bees and flowers and trees and other creatures of the forest. Then humans developed self-consciousness—the sense of ego-centeredness which cut them off from Nature. They couldn't be in Nature as before, but they could step aside and observe it objectively. Observation led to knowledge, knowledge to power, and power too often corrupted. Where once we existed within the rhythms of the natural world, we increasingly forgot that we were part of that world, and instead attempted to control it, as if we were more important than Nature. But to Tom Bombadil, who existed before Nature even took form, all of our deeds are simply silly little games that pass away while Nature endures.

Frodo begins to realize that he has no category in which to include Tom Bombadil; he is more than anything Frodo has even considered can exist in the world. He asks "who are you, Master?"[167] And Tom tells him that he is "Eldest. . . . Tom was here before the first raindrop and the first acorn. He was here before the Kings and the graves and the Barrow-wights. When he Elves passed westward, Tom was here already, before the seas were bent. He knew the dark under ths stars when it was fearless—before the Dark Lord came from Outside."[168]

Thus Tom was there before anything that existed. We earlier characterized Bombadil as a force of nature beyond human definition, but he seems to be more yet. Perhaps he might best be seen as Nature before nature forms. And note that he is benevolent! Over the course of his journey, Frodo will be wounded by darkness, a darkness that seems like it will swallow everything good and pure, but somehow he find a way back to the natural world he loves so much: best represented by the Shire. His task will be to chew on the darkness long enough that eventually he can come back to the light with what he has learned from the darkness. And he must never forget Tom Bombadil, and his innate goodness, a reminder that before everything that man created, there was already good in the world.

Having told tales all through the day, Goldberry returns from her washing, and all have another enormous dinner together. Afterwards they listen to Goldberry singing songs that create pictures in their minds. Then she goes off to bed and leaves Tom to ask them questions. He already knows much of their situation and soon has pulled the rest out of them. Knowing all, he asks to see the Ring. Frodo is surprised to find himself taking it off its chain and handing it to Tom, who looks through it with a laugh, then slips in on his finger. And, unlike Frodo and everyone else on Middle-Earth, he does not disappear: Tom remains Tom, unchanged by the Ring. He takes it off and tosses it in the air, where it disappears. Before Frodo can react, the Ring has reappeared and Tom hands it to Frodo. Tom has no interest in such things, but Frodo is a doubting Thomas, wondering if Tom has played some trick on him. So Frodo puts on the Ring, (for the first time in the book) and vanishes from everyone's sight. Everyone, that is, except Tom: when Frodo sneaks toward the door, Bombadil tells him to come back and take off the Ring. He looks better without it. Stay and talk a while longer.

Tom Bombadil is not bound by laws that affect humans and Hobbits, Elves and Dwarves and Wizards. The One Ring, so powerful that the fate of Middle Earth hangs on a balance because of its very existence, is for Tom only a pretty piece of jewelry. It has no effect on him: he doesn't vanish, he doesn't stop seeing Frodo when Frodo vanishes from the other's sight. Tom exists in a reality more primary that the reality within which all the others live.

The next morning the Hobbits are off again, with directions from Tom, and a warning not to fool with the barrow wights. And he also leaves them with a song to sing if, despite his warnings, they get into trouble. Off they go. Throughout the morning, they seem to make good progress, but when they stop for lunch, once again they grow careless. They lean against a cool standing stone to rest and lunch. After a Hobbit-sized meal, they find themselves taking a Hobbit nap, just as if they were still safe in the Shire. But they are not safe in the Shire: when they waken, the sun is setting and everywhere around them is thick fog. It is already too late for a safe passage through the barrows. In the fog, the company becomes separated, and one by one, they are mesmerized and taken underground by the Barrow-wights, the ghosts who guard the treasures hidden within their barrows. When Frodo awakens, he finds himself imprisoned inside a barrow, under the earth, under the spell of a Barrow-wight. H can see Sam, Pippin, and Merry all lying as if dead. Everywhere about them lie treasures of gold and jewels. The three have been dressed in white and adorned with such treasures. Most ominously a sword lies across all three necks.

He hears a cold song, a chant of death. Then he sees a hideous arm walking on its fingers toward Sam, ready to seize the sword that lies across the necks of the Hobbits. Though he briefly considers putting on the Ring and escaping, Frodo would never leave his friends to this awful fate. Pulling his hand back out of his pocket, where it had involuntarily begun reaching for the Ring, Frodo finds the strength to grab a nearby sword and hack off the hand. The sword shatters, a Barrow-wight screams and the little light there was in the barrow is extinguished.

Once again we see that Frodo is special. Whereas the other Hobbits lie as if dead, Frodo alone wakes and observes his surroundings. Though his fear is great and there is a temptation to put on the Ring and escape, instead he finds the courage to protect his friends.

At this moment of urgency, Frodo remembers the song Tom Bombadil told him to sing if he were ever in need of his help. When he sings, Tom, who has no fear of Barrow-wights (or for that matter, of anything else), comes to their rescue. Tom sings the Barrow-wights out of their own barrow, never to return. He and Frodo carry the others to safety. Then Tom goes back inside and comes back carrying some of the treasure. He sings the three mesmerized Hobbits back to life. They are startled, at first not remembering who they are, filled instead with memories of the dead in whose home they had lain. As usual, Sam is the first to bring things back to normalcy—he wants to know what happened to his clothes?

Every time there is trouble Tom appears, and each time he sings to take away the evil. his seems to be a truth that song heals at the very deepest level. And what is song? The merging of word and music. One of the famous phrases in the New Testament of the Christian Bible is "In the beginning was the Word, and the Word was with God, and the Word was God" (John 1:1). A little later in is gospel, John adds that "The Word was made flesh and dwelt among us" (John 1:14). Let's ignore the religious interpretation of this and simply view it as a beautiful way to say that words are where the human meets the divine. And throughout all human history the sacred has been expressed in words set to music. In Sam's chapter, we saw how when Frodo was tied up in the tower by the Orcs, it was Sam's spontaneously composed song that led him to Frodo. And when the Hobbit's were trapped in the barrow, it was Frodo singing Tom's song that brought Tom to their aid.

Tom tells them to stop worrying about silly things like clothes when they have barely escaped with their lives. He leaves them to recover while he goes off to find their ponies. The Hobbits dress themselves in spare clothing from the packs on the ponies, then Tom gives them each a dagger taken from the treasure trove to serve as swords for the Hobbits.

It is one of these daggers, forged by the Great Men of the earlier ages, that Merry much later uses to stab the Lord of the Nazgûls before he can kill Éowyn!

Dressed and armed, mounted on their ponies, the Hobbits are finally ready to make their way back to the road. Given the troubles they've experienced so far, Bombadil decides to accompany them to the road that will lead toward The Prancing Pony. When they reach the road, they try to persuade him to accompany them to the inn, but Tom says that "Tom's country ends here: he will not pass the borders. Tom has his house to mind, and Goldberry is waiting."[169]

> *There are limits to Tom's domain. And undoubtedly it has shrunk over time, as Middle Earth has lost its contact with the natural world. And that is why we have spent so much time talking about Frodo's experience of Tom Bombadil. This may seem like an innocent interlude in the story, but it's of the essence in understanding Frodo's task and the pain he carries with him. The world of the Shire which he loved so much and which he left to carry the Ring, is a world where Hobbits still exist in harmony with nature. The world that Sauron would create is one where everything natural is destroyed, just as Saruman destroys the trees in order to create the machinery of death Sauron needs. In Tom Bombadil, we see Nature before Nature took the forms we see all about us. We talk about Mother Nature, but Tom is Father Nature. Within his world there can be both good and evil, since man's moral judgements do not yet apply, but there is nothing of the evil that only comes with man's existence. At its base, the darkness with which Frodo will struggle is the absence of Tom and the natural world, the inability to connect with that world. And we've been given the clue that it is song that is the essence of that world. Frodo doesn't sing many songs as his journey grows darker.*

WOUNDED BY DARKNESS

Because Frodo is the central figure in *The Lord of the Rings*, we have heard much of Frodo's story through his interactions with our other heros in earlier chapters. For example, in Aragorn's chapter, the Path of the King, we saw how Frodo foolishly put on the Ring in the Inn of the Prancing Pony. Warned by Strider of the danger facing him, Frodo is at first put off by this dark, menacing stranger. But, regardless of the frightening outer appearance Strider presents to Frodo and his friends, it is Frodo who first recognizes Strider as someone to be trusted. While Sam worries that he might be one of Sauron's spies, Frodo sees through Strider's rough exterior to the greatness within and says that "I think one of his [i.e., Sauron's] spies would—well, seem fairer and feel fouler, if you understand."[170] Even this early in his own development, Frodo is able to recognize the good in others, even when the good is hidden from view. This is an ability that will stand him in good stead many times over the course of his journey, most especially with Gollum.

Though at this point, Strider leads the company, it is already Frodo who is the center, the person for whom Strider would give his life.

> *Once we are on our journey, if it is a true journey to which we have been called, we have to trust our instincts, our sense of what and who is good or bad. Time and again we will need to make choices despite our seemingly more rational self telling us that this doesn't make any sense at all. We need different guides on an inner journey.*

With Strider leading the way and the Black Riders not far behind, the journey soon becomes much darker. Despite Strider's skill at taking a circuitous path through the wilderness on the way to the Elven kingdom of Rivendell, the party is forced to stop on Weathertop, where they hoped, in vain, to find Gandalf. During the night they are attacked by five of the Black Riders, including their leader, the Lord of the Nazgûls. In his terror as they crowd around him, Frodo makes a terrible mistake: he puts on the Ring, which causes him to enter the nether-world where the Ring-Wraiths truly live, where they can now see him. The leader stabs Frodo with a poisoned sword—one might almost say he stabs him with darkness. At this desperate moment, Frodo does the right thing and removes the ring, just before losing consciousness. Aragorn fights like a demon and drives the Black Riders away before they can kill Frodo and steal the Ring.

Poisoned by the wound, in the days that follow Frodo grows progressively more ill. Only Strider's knowledge of herb lore keeps him alive, but, at this stage of Strider's own development, his power and skill is insufficient to do more than buy time until they can get to Rivendell. Once Frodo crosses the ford and enters the kingdom of Rivendell, a combination of Elrond 's and Gandalf's magical powers swallow up the Black Riders in a raging flood, saving him. But, though Elrond is healing powers are great enough to be able to save Frodo's life, this wound will never be fully healed. A portion of darkness, of Sauron's kingdom, has entered into Frodo, where it will eat away at him forever.

> *None of us is perfect, we all make mistakes, often big mistakes, especially in the early parts of our journey. And sometimes those mistakes might, seen within a bigger picture, be necessary. Though Frodo's fear leads him to put on the Ring, and that leads him to be stabbed with darkness, it is just that connection with darkness that gives him such pity later for Gollum. And without Gollum, the Ring would never have been destroyed. We all have to be wounded in order to grow to a new level. It is that open wound that is our connection to deeper things.*

In some ways, Frodo's journey really starts at this point. It is no surprise that at the Council of Elrond, while the others are squabbling over the impossibility of destroying the Ring, it is Frodo who offers to carry it the rest of the way: "I will take the Ring, though I do not know the way."[171] Nor is it surprising that Elrond immediately acknowledges him as the proper Ring bearer: "I think this task is appointed for you, Frodo; and that if you do not find a way, no one will."[172] After all, Frodo alone has been a Ring bearer already, and Frodo alone has been wounded by the darkness. Who else to carry the ring to Mount Doom?

> *Elrond is presented as the male counterpoint to Galadriel. Both can see deeply into others, though perhaps Galadriel sees deeper. Both have foreknowledge of what is to come, and perhaps her Elrond sees farther. So he already sees Frodo's quality long before the others (save Gandalf) do. And he sees how events will unfold, with Frodo at the center of those events.*

Carrying both the Ring without, and the darkness within, Frodo is never free from further attacks by various of Sauron's minions. Whether Black Riders or Orcs or other darker forces, they always recognize Frodo as the important person in the group, the one who must be captured and taken to Sauron. Intelligence is not a factor; darkness speaks to darkness.

For example, outside the Mines of Moria, a giant squid-like sea creature singles out Frodo from the group. It grabs Frodo's foot with one of its tentacles and begins to drag him into the water. When Sam slashes at the tentacle and frees Frodo, the entire company flees into the mines. Foiled in his attempt to capture Frodo, the sea creature pulls the massive doors closed, then blocks the entrance with boulders and uprooted trees. The company is now trapped in the dark of the mines, where other creatures can make their attempt to capture Frodo and the Ring. Deep in the catacombs, the company is attacked by a horde of Orcs, whose leader somehow knows to attack Frodo. He stabs Frodo with a spear, seemingly killing him. But he is not dead—when Frodo left Rivendell, it was with two great gifts from Bilbo: his sword Sting and a vest made of mithril. It is this mithril vest, worth a king's ransom, that saves Frodo. So, just as powerful forces are at work in an attempt to bring Frodo and the Ring to Sauron, so too are powerful forces at work to protect him. And none more powerful than Galadriel. Thus Frodo is the place where both darkness and light meet.

And in our individual inner journeys, we live at just that critical balance point between light and dark, conscious and unconscious, good and bad.

THE MIRROR OF GALADRIEL

When the company is brought before Celeborn and Galadriel in Lothlórien, Galadriel looks into each of their souls. She stares directly at Frodo as she tells the company that "your Quest stands upon the edge of a knife. Stray but a little and it will fail, to the ruin of all. Yet hope remains while the Company is true."[173]

Though Galadriel might not see the future as clearly as Elrond, she sees exactly what the state of things is at any point in time. We need to appeal to both the Elrond and the Galadriel within us for knowledge along the way.

After spending some time in her kingdom recovering their strength and their spirit, one evening Galadriel silently beckons Frodo and Sam to follow her. She leads them into an enclosed garden, down a flight of stairs into an enclosed green glade, through which a silver stream runs.

In the middle stands a pedestal with a silver on top, with a silver vase beside it. All is green or silver in Galadriel's world! She uses the silver vase to capture the silver water and fill the silver basin. Then she asks them if they want to look within. We have already discussed the vision of a decimated Shire that Sam saw in Galadriel's Mirror. Poor Sam wishes he had never asked to see Elf magic.

When she asks Frodo, wise Frodo asks whether she advises him to do so. But Galadriel only brings people to her Mirror; it is up to them whether or not they look. So Frodo gazes into the mirror and sees the figure of a wizard approaching. It might be Gandalf, but the wizard is dressed all in white, with a white staff, and Gandalf the Grey is dead. The wizard's head is bowed too low for Frodo to be sure who it is: Gandalf? Saruman? Only later will he find this is a vision of the reborn Gandalf who Frodo will meet again only after fulfilling his Quest.

He then sees Bilbo stirring about in his room. His papers are disordered and outside it's raining. Thus a picture of discord with one he loves the most.

The Mirror begins to show him deeper things. He sees scenes that he realizes are part of the great sweep of history that has led to this point, where Frodo now takes his place in history.

He sees a great storm at Sea. Though he has never seen the Sea, he knows it instantly. Out of the West comes a tall black ship. Though he doesn't know it now, this is the ship Aragorn will use to save Minis Tirith from falling.

And then, in horror Frodo sees the Eye of Sauron growing ever larger in the Mirror, searching in every direction for the One Ring, the Ring Frodo carries on a chain around his neck. As he watches, the Ring grows so heavy that it pulls him down toward the water in the bowl. It is only when he hears Galadriel's voice telling him not to touch the water that the Eye fades away and Frodo finds himself once more in the green glade. Freed from the Eye, he looks to Galadriel and sees a ring on her finger, a ring that reflects the light of the stars, and he knows that she, too, is a ring-bearer, one who wears one of the three great rings given to the Elves.

So like meets like, even if the comparison of a great Elf queen with a little Hobbit, might seem strange. When the field is narrowed to those who are ring-bearers, there are very few who know what it means: Sauron and Elrond and Galadriel and Frodo and, briefly in the future, Sam. And, of course, Gollum! On our own journey, we find that the number of people who are also on the journey narrows the farther we go.

Frodo, ever aware of greatness when he encounters it, offers the One Ring to Galadriel, admitting that his task is probably too much for him.. She laughs and tells him: "In place of the Dark Lord you will set up a Queen. And I shall not be dark, but beautiful and terrible as the Morning and the Night! . . . All shall love me and despair"[174] As she talks, she grows taller and even more beautiful, if that is possible. Then she laughs again, rejects the Ring and becomes the Galadriel that all love, in her simplicity and earthly beauty. "I pass the test. I will diminish, and go into the West, and remain Galadriel."[175] Yes, she passes the test, as did Gandalf and Aragorn before her, and as will Faramir after her.

As they leave the green glade, Frodo asks why it is, since he wears the One Ring, that he cannot look into the minds of all the other ring-bearers. Galadriel tells him that he could, but that it requires such great power that the attempt would destroy him. But that, regardless, he has indeed grown more perceptive: he has seen deeply into her thoughts; he has seen the Eye; he has seen the ring upon her finger. At that she turns to Sam and asks if he saw the ring and he confesses that he wondered what in the world they were talking about as he only saw star light on her finger. And good, simple Sam tells her that he wishes she'd take Frodo up on his offer and accept the Ring. He knows she'd "put things to rights."[176] But Galadriel knows that over time, the Ring would be too great a temptation even for her. Frodo and Sam leave together, each having learned perhaps more than they want to know.

FRODO AND BOROMIR

Galadriel has already seen into Boromir's heart and knows how he lusts for the Ring and the power it carries, power he thinks he can use wisely to defend his beloved Minis Tirith. But she is wise enough to know that it is not her place to stop events before they happen; they must unfold in their own time. When the company leaves Lothlórien, none is sure where they will go next: West with Boromir toward Minis Tirith or East toward Mordor? They are able to put off the decision for a while by going down the Great River which for a distance at least is common to both choices. But eventually they come to a place where a choice must be made and the burden of the choice lies on Frodo. He asks for an hour to be alone with his thoughts before he gives his decision.

Frodo needing time alone to collect his thoughts is reminiscent of the story of Jesus in Gethsemane on the night before he was taken in custody. Both Jesus and Frodo would like their burden to be lifted from them, as would be all. But once you've started on your path, you have to carry the burden no matter where it takes you.

But Boromir is afraid that the decision has already been made to go East toward Mordor, so he follows Frodo and confronts him, at his smiling best, using all his skills of persuasion to convince Frodo to give him the Ring. When Frodo reminds him of the Council of Elrond, when all agreed that the power of the Ring was too great to be borne by anyone, Boromir's true intentions become clear. Such power belongs not to Elves or Hobbits or sly Wizards, but to "truehearted men" like himself, men strong enough to carry any burden, powerful enough to know that one has to be ruthless when fighting an enemy such as Sauron. But Boromir is a warrior not a diplomat, he soon loses his temper with this silly Hobbit who would deliver the Ring right into Sauron's hands.

When he leaps at Frodo trying to grab the Ring, Frodo puts on the Ring for the fourth time. He had done this for the first time out of suspicion with Tom Bombadil, for the second out of foolishness in the Prancing Pony, when he did not yet know its full power. And he put in on for the third time upon Weathertop in a desperate attempt to escape from the Black Riders. But that only allowed them to see him all the better, and led to a wound of darkness that he would carry forever. This time it is necessary to take the risk in order to preserve the Ring from Boromir. With the strange sight that the Ring gives, he sees war coming from all directions, all under the control of Sauron. And then the Eye of Sauron seeks him, calling him. An inner voice, Gandalf's voice tells him to take off the Ring. For the first time, Frodo realizes that he is not under the control (at least yet) of either the Eye or the Voice. He has a choice and he decided to take off the Ring, just in time before Sauron would have had him under his control.

The farther Frodo goes on his quest, the greater temptation the Ring presents, and the greater possibility for evil if he yields to that temptation. The path always narrows as we advance.

FRODO FULFILS HIS DESTINY

The company now splits into three parts: Merry and Pippin taken by the Orcs; Aragorn, Legolas and Gimli in hot pursuit, hoping to save the young Hobbits; and Frodo and Sam off on their journey toward Mordor. Boromir lies dead and Gandalf is still thought to be dead. At this point, Frodo's quest appears doomed. Thankfully, he has Sam, with his never-to-be-quelled optimism, as companion. Frodo simply accepts the near certainty of failure, but nevertheless, moves forward toward Mordor. This is his task and he will do it, regardless of the consequences for himself. He only hates that Sam is forced to accept the same fate.

Much of Frodo's story from this point has been told in previous two chapters: The Path of Tragic Failure (Gollum) and The Path of Love (Sam). We watched how Frodo's kindness brought Sméagol (Gollum's original personality) into consciousness, and Sméagol and Gollum battled for control of the personality. For a while, Sméagol was in the ascendent and did everything he could to help Frodo (even if it meant also helping the "nasty Hobbit" Sam). But when Frodo was forced to trick Sméagol so that Faramir's men could take him alive, Gollum convinced Sméagol that even Frodo must die. We know that Frodo was saving his life, but to Sméagol/Gollum, it was treachery.

Gollum then led Frodo and Sam into the great she-Spider Shelob's lair, confident that She woul devour them, as she had so many before. Afterwards, Gollum could pick through the carcasses and take the Ring for himself. Frodo's bravery at first drove Shelob away, but then she came back and stung Frodo into seeming death. Sam stabbed Shelob and drove her away for good. Afterwards, heartsick, convinced Frodo was dead, Sam himself took the Ring in order to try and complete the quest. When he found that Frodo was not dead, he rescuesdFrodo (with a song! Tom Bombadil taught them well) and the two Hobbits moved on to the last stages of their journey. Finally on Mount Doom, when the moment came to throw the Ring into the volcano, Frodo was unable to relinquish it. Its hold on him had grown too strong, as it was for everyone who ever carried it. He cried out that "I have come, but I do not choose now to do what I came to do. I will not do this deed. The Ring is mine!"[177] Gollum then fulfilled his tragic destiny, biting off Frodo's finger and falling into the volcano with the Ring.

Sometimes, in order to finish a great task, it is necessary to sacrifice a part of ourselves.

All that we have told before. And now, just like that Sauron's kingdom comes to an end. His mighty tower falls, the Great Gate falls, all fall down, as if they were all the toys of a child, and the child had grown weary of this game.

Ultimately that is what all of Sauron's plans are: a child's game, in this case an evil child's game. Often, when we finally complete our task, we find that all that we struggled with now seems only an illusion, only a house of cards. We can no longer remember why it was all so hard.

And Frodo is Frodo again, as he has not been since he has carried the burden of the Ring. Sam is overjoyed to see his master finally at peace, and then, sad that he has nothing to bind Frodo's mangled hand. Frodo is filled with compassion for Gollum, the compassion only one Ring-bearer can feel for another. As he and Sam lie in peace, "But for him, Sam, I could not have not have destroyed the Ring. The Quest would have been in vain, even at the bitter end. So let us forgive him! For the Quest is achieved, and now all is over. I am glad you are here with me. Here at the end of all things, Sam."[178]

But while this is the end of Sauron's reign, it is not "the end of all things." Strider/Aragorn is crowned King Elessar of Gondor, and weds Arwen Evenstar, to rule in peace and prosperity for one hundred twenty years. After the celebration of the wedding, when the Hobbits are ready to return to the Shire, Queen Arwen has a great gift for Frodo: since she has chosen to live as a mortal with Aragorn, she gives Frodo her place on the ship that will take the Elves across the Sea to the Undying Lands. But before he goes, we need to look at Frodo's return to the Shire in order to see how Frodo has been changed by his quest.

AFTER THE END OF THE QUEST

We have seen in the Chapter on The Path of Curiosity how Merry and Pippin took the lead in the Battle of Bywater, in which the Hobbits regained control of the Shire from Sharkey's men. During the battle, Frodo remains above the fray, his only admonition being that they must not slay any Hobbits, even if they have become collaborators. And during the battle, he prevents the Hobbits from killing any of their enemies who throw down their weapons. With the battle won, it is finally time to confront the leader of the ruffians: Sharkey.

And who do they find when they meet Sharkey: Saruman! Saruman, who, even in defeat, gloats over how he has destroyed their lovely village. Frodo tells him sternly to leave and never return, but the other Hobbits thirst for blood and want to kill him. Saruman turns as always to his twisted tongue, warning them that he still has power and any who kill him will be cursed, and his blood on the Shire will curse it forever. Only Frodo has no fear of Saruman. He tells the other Hobbits that Saruman's only remaining power lies in his ability to make them believe his lies. But, nevertheless, they aren't to harm Saruman. "It is useless to meet revenge with revenge: it will heal nothing."[179] He again bids Saruman to be on his way.

Saruman calls Wormtongue to follow him, then, as he passes Frodo, pulls out a hidden knife and stabs Frodo. To no avail, as Frodo is still wearing chain-mail. Even this is not enough for Frodo to allow the others to kill Saruman. He says: "He was great once, of a noble kind that we should not dare to raise our hands against. He is fallen and his cure is beyond us; but I would still spare him, in the hope that he may find it."[180] Even Saruman is stunned by Frodo's words, telling him "you are wise, and cruel. You have robbed my revenge of sweetness, and now I must go hence in bitterness, in debt to your mercy. I hate it and you!"[181]

Frodo now sees as deeply as Galadriel. He can look deep inside Saruman and see what once was there, what might still be there if only Saruman could lay aside his arrogance and his cruelty. And Saruman, like Boromir before him, cannot stand to be seen as he is and was and still could be, preferring the face he chooses to present to the world.

With that, he turns on his heel to leave. When Wormtongue hesitantly starts to follow him, Frodo tells Grima Wormtongue that he knows of no evil that he has done him, and that he may remain until he feels ready to leave. Saruman laughs at the idea that Wormtongue is guiltless and tells everyone that Wormtongue killed Lotho, the Hobbit who collaborated with Sharkey's men to rule the Shire. When Wormtongue reminds Saruman that he did the killing at his insistence, Saruman laughs and kicks him in the face as he lies before him on the ground. This is too much: Wormtongue snaps, draws a knife, and slits Saruman's throat. Instantly three Hobbits pull their bows and kill him, thus bringing an end to the last remaining villains of *The Lord of the Rings*.

As the Hobbits begin the restoration of the Shire, Frodo willingly goes into seclusion, writing the history of the quest, much as Bilbo had before him. To the villagers, who have heard nothing but vague rumors of the goings-on that happened in the great world, Merry and Pippin, who led the fight against Sharkey's men, become heroes. And Sam, too, though he is too modest to notice. But Frodo is overlooked by the villagers, since they have no way to understand someone such as Frodo has become.

Frodo's fate is inevitable. People recognize warriors and kings, people who can strut before them. It is much more difficult to recognize greatness in quiet dignity. And few, if any, can understand what it means to carry darkness inside in order to protect others. And though Sam feels badly for Frodo, by this time, it would not even occur to Frodo that he should be recognized for his deeds. And if he was, he wouldn't welcome the recognition. His task is now to record what has happened for the future.

For Frodo has been wounded for all time, in part by the blade of the Lord of the Nazgûls, in larger part, simply by bearing the burden of the Ring. There is no home left in Middle Earth for Frodo. He has looked too deeply into the face of darkness. Darkness has passed inside him, and until he can bring lightness out of that dark, he will remain wounded. Somehow he has to find a way back to the world of nature he found in Tom Bombadil's little world, though he passed far from Bombadil's reign. Just as Tom sang of the world that was and remains, Frodo has to discover a song within himself, a song that can sing of the new world to come.

At the end of *The Lord of the Rings*, Frodo has not yet found a way to heal that wound. He takes passage with Bilbo and Gandalf and the Elves on the ship that will take them to the Undying Lands, where he will live forever, but be no more at peace than he is in Middle Earth. Frodo's destiny, like that of Jesus and Buddha, is to bear the burden for others until they are able to bear it for themselves.

Appendix

Tom Shippey has called John Ronald Reuel Tolkien "*the* author of the century."[182] And his masterwork, *The Lord of the Rings*, vies with a very small number of other books - Joyce's *Ulysses*? Orwell's 1984? - as *the* book of the century. As the twenty-first century begins, it appears that its popularity and appeal may, if anything, rise still higher. Even before the current hugely successful movie series began, *The Lord of the Rings* had sold over 50 million copies worldwide. It has been translated into virtually every modern language, including such unexpected ones as Catalan, Estonian, and Vietnamese. If you add in Tolkien's other books, especially the two most closely related to *The Lord of the Rings* - the children's book *The Hobbit* and the dense scholarly *The Silmarillion* - Tolkien has sold over 100 million copies.[183]

Of this enormous popularity, Tolkien once wrote a reader: "Being a cult figure in one's own lifetime I am afraid is not at all pleasant. However I do not find that it tends to puff one up; in my case at any rate it makes be feel extremely small and inadequate. But even the nose of a very modest idol cannot remain untickled by the sweet smell of incense."[184] He did, however, like the financial security his books' sales provided and once ingenuously told a younger friend: "I've been a poor man all my life, but now for the first time I've a lot of money. Would you like some?"[185]

As one might expect with any book so popular, *The Lord of the Rings* has polarized readers and critics, who either love it or hate it, with very little reaction in-between. Those who hate it find all this nonsense about Hobbits and Elves, and Dwarves and wizards childish. They characterize the clear moral dichotomy it draws between the light and the dark as overly simplistic in a time when the morality of "serious fiction" is more often grey and ambiguous. Perhaps most telling, the overall concept of a hero's quest is considered to be proper subject matter only for children's books, with little or no resonance for adults. Yet resonance it has for those who respond to it.

THE FEAR OF DRAGONS

Ursula K. Le Guin, author of science-fiction, fantasy, children's books, and herself an admirer of *The Lord of the Rings*, wrote an essay, "The Fear of Dragons,"[186] about the fear Americans have of fantasy. She opened her essay with a telling anecdote about a friend who had gone to look for a copy of *The Hobbit* in the children's section of her local library. The librarian told her friend "Oh, we keep that in the adult collection; we don't feel that escapism is good for children." Le Guin goes on to add that "was merely reflecting, in perfect good faith, something that goes very deep in the American character: a moral disapproval of fantasy, a disapproval so intense, and often so aggressive, that I cannot help but see it as arising, fundamentally, from fear."[187]

Why fear fantasy rather than simply disregard it as childish and/or insignificant? After all, much of the overt criticism of *The Lord of the Rings* is, on the surface, merely dismissive, though the extremes of scorn are telling. We are accustomed to supposed "serious" literature mirroring the world around us, and our morally ambiguous values within that world. Fiction with plot, likeable characters, and especially strong moral values is automatically relegated to genre categories such as science fiction or mysteries.

Tolkien had little patience with critics who accuse fantasy of being escapist. At about the same time he began to write *The Lord of the Rings*, he wrote a now-famed essay "On Fairy Stories," in which he argued that "not only do they confound the escape of the prisoner with the flight of the deserter, but they would seem to prefer the acquiescence of 'the quisling' to the resistance of the patriot."[188] Turning their argument on its head, he said that so-called "'serious' literature is often no more than play under a glass roof by the side of a municipal swimming-bath. Fairy-stories may invent monsters that fly in the air or dwell in the deep, but at least they do not try to escape from heaven or the sea."[189]

In fact, rather than feeling defensive about the value of fantasy, Tolkien felt that fantasy was the highest, purest form of Art—the form that could have the most impact on the imagination. He saw no conflict between fantasy and reason; he insisted that "the keener and clearer is the reason, the better fantasy will it make."[190] A good work of fantasy presents a portrait of an alternative reality that, despite differences from our own world, or perhaps because of those differences, may force us to step back and look critically at the world in which we live. And this can be deeply troubling.

Le Guin understood this well, and in speaking of *The Lord of the Rings*, argued that "that it is told in the language of fantasy is not an accident, or because Tolkien is an escapist, or because he was writing for children. It is a fantasy because fantasy is the natural, the appropriate language for the recounting of the spiritual journey and the struggle of good and evil in the soul. (p. 64).

Tolkien was a deeply religious Catholic. For him, the description in Genesis was significant: "God created man in His own image; in the image of God He created him; male and female He created them" (1:27). In the creation of fantasy, Tolkien felt that we come closest to reflecting that parentage. In nearly poetic terms he pleaded that "fantasy remains a human right: we make in our measure and in our derivative mode, because we are made: and not only made, but made in the image and likeness of a Maker."[191]

With proper humility, he felt that the proper role of the writer of fantasy was to be a "sub-creator," one who creates new fictional worlds. It is incumbent on the writer to make those worlds as inwardly consistent and detailed as possible, so that the reader can explore them to any desired depth without running into inconsistencies. A world of fantasy should be 3-dimensional like the real world, not a flat stage set in which, if you look from behind the curtains, you see that it is only made of cardboard. In Tolkien's view, if God could create the immensity of the world, and we shared in His divinity, we had the capacity within us for a level of creativity that went far beyond simply aping the world we saw around us. Rather it was incumbent upon us as sub-creators to look to deeper realities inside ourselves and then to make our best attempt to fully capture those realities in print. Tolkien achieved that goal to an extent unequaled in literature. Though a deep spirituality suffused his work, it emerged naturally out of the depth of the world he created, not from any overt presentation of his particular religious beliefs. This contrasted with the work of his best friend, C. S. Lewis, as we will see next.

ALLEGORY VS. SYMBOL

Tolkien received his degree from Oxford, then, like most British men of his generation, served in World War I. The horrors he saw in that war were to have a lasting impact on Tolkien and his work. After the war, he worked for two years on the Oxford English dictionary. Of that time, he said that "I learned more in those two years than in any other equal period of my life."[192] As enriching as this time was for Tolkien, it was essentially a part-time job that barely paid the bills. In late 1920, at the age of 28, he became a professor and remained one for the rest of his life, first at the University of Leeds, and then as Professor of Anglo-Saxon at Oxford.

In 1925, when Tolkien returned to Oxford, the English School (what we in America would call the English Department) was divided into two opposing camps: Language and Literature. Language actually meant philology, and so, of course, Tolkien was part of the language faction, and wary of those in Literature. The following year, a young man named Clive Staples Lewis was elected Fellow and Tutor in English Language and Literature, hence on the other side of the divide. Despite this, Tolkien and C. S. Lewis ("Jack" to Tolkien and his other friends) became fast friends, in large part due to their joint interest in Anglo-Saxon.

They complemented each other well. Lewis was a large, cocky extravert. Tolkien, who was smaller and shyer and always a little prone to self-doubt, undoubtedly needed someone like Lewis in his life. Both were men who enjoyed, and spent a great deal of time in, the company of other men, a commonplace of the time for upper-class males to a degree which is hard for us now to appreciate. Though Tolkien had a long and largely happy marriage, he was always to feel more comfortable with men than with women.

Tolkien and Lewis read and commented on each other's work as it developed. Though Tolkien valued his opinion highly, he never accepted any of Lewis' suggested changes to his work. Either he left the work as is without comment, or he rewrote it entirely, a habit that was never to change for Tolkien. As Lewis said, "no one every influenced Tolkien – you might as well try to influence an bandersnatch."[193] Lewis was more important to Tolkien for his friendly support than for any editorial or critical assistance he could provide, as Tolkien freely admitted: "The unpayable debit that I owe him was not 'influence' as it is ordinarily understood, but sheer encouragement. He was for long my only audience. Only from him did I ever get the idea that my 'stuff' could be more than a private hobby."[194]

Lewis had been brought up Protestant with a dislike of Catholics, then became agnostic in his teens. He found more spiritual sustenance in pagan mythologies, which for him contained something great and nourishing, but which he did not have to believe in literally. Inevitably, given Tolkien's vast knowledge of mythology, coupled with his staunch Catholicism, the two talked at great length about religion and its relationship to mythology. Tolkien slowly chipped away at Lewis' somewhat naive beliefs until, in 1929, Lewis gave way and professed a belief in God (though not yet in Christianity and certainly not in Catholicism). Two years later, twelve days after a memorable late night walk and discussion with Tolkien and a joint friend (Hugo Dyson), Lewis decided that he now accepted Christianity (though he was never to become Catholic, as Tolkien had really hoped). The deciding factor seems to have been Tolkien's argument that Lewis was being unreasonable in accepting the essential truth captured in the mythology of non-Christian religions, while denying it within Christianity.[195]

With Lewis' conversion to Christianity, their friendship deepened still more, though Tolkien always felt saddened that, instead of converting to Catholicism, Lewis reverted to the religion of his youth. "He would not re-enter Christianity by a new door, but by the old one:

at least in the sense that in taking it up again he would also take up again, or reawaken, the prejudices so sedulously planned in childhood and boyhood."[196] By the mid-forties, though Tolkien still regarded Lewis as his closest friend, he was troubled by the fame Lewis was acquiring for his popular books on Christianity such as *The Problem of Pain* and *The Screwtape Letters*. Tolkien, who considered Lewis' theological views to be simplistic, referred to him disparagingly as "Everyman's Theologian."[197]

Tolkien grew still more disappointed when, in 1949, Lewis began to read him the first of his "Narnia" stories: *The Lion, the Witch and the Wardrobe*. By this time, *The Lord of the Rings* was nearing completion (though it would not be until 1954 that the first volume, *The Fellowship of the Ring*, would be truly completed and published). Lewis (and others in a group called "The Inklings") had heard every hard-won page of what was to be *The Lord of the Rings* read out loud by Tolkien. Though Lewis was enthusiastic about much of it, he also offered criticism (especially of the poetry) that often offended Tolkien (though, as we have already said, such criticism did not in any way dissuade Tolkien from the path he was taking). Now Lewis was writing his own fantasy novels, knocking them off them at lightning speed, with little or no deliberation or forethought.

The result, to Tolkien, was a hideous hodgepodge of incompatible parts, in his words "about as bad as can be."[198] Lewis was merely pulling in sources wherever they occurred to him, from Father Christmas to Dryads, and throwing them all into the pot. It was absolutely the opposite of Tolkien's own belief that a fantasy should create a world that was internally as consistent as (or perhaps even more consistent than) the world we live in. And worst of all, these stories were not really stories at all; they were *allegories*, in which Lewis preached thinly disguised sermons on his (to Tolkien's mind) vacuous version of Christianity. As this growing series of books became enormously popular, at a time when Tolkien was himself still struggling with the completion of his own mammoth work, inevitably he found himself somewhat estranged from Lewis, and was never to fully recover their deep friendship of earlier years. But Lewis never seemed to notice, and, happily for both, their friendship never faded entirely.

Allegory is a literary, dramatic, or pictorial device in which each literal character, object, and event represents a symbol illustrating an idea or moral or religious principle. Some critics have confused archetypal symbolism, which emerges ineluctably from within a true fantasy, with allegorical symbolism, which is imposed from without by the author. Some have argued, for example, that *The Lord of the Rings* is an allegory for the struggle against Hitler in World War II. Tolkien disagreed strongly, insisting that he was writing a story and nothing more. In the introduction to *The Lord of the Rings*, Tolkien remarks that:

> I cordially dislike allegory in all its manifestations, and always have done so since I grew old and wary enough to detect its presence. I much prefer history, true or feigned, with its varied applicability to the thought and experience of readers. I think many confuse 'applicability' with 'allegory'; but the one resides in the freedom of the reader, and the other in the purposed domination of the author.[199]

Tolkien's view accords closely with what psychologist C. G. Jung called the "symbolic attitude: a view "which *assigns meaning* to events, whether great or small, and attaches to this meaning a greater value than to bare facts."[200] Jung contrasted the symbolic attitude with the semiotic and the allegorical:

> The concept of a *symbol* should in my view be strictly distinguished from that of a *sign*. . . . Every view which interprets the symbolic expression as an analogue or an abbreviated designation for a *known* thing is *semiotic*. A view which interprets the symbolic expression as the best possible formulation of a relatively *unknown* thing, which for that reason cannot be more clearly or characteristically represented is *symbolic*. A view which interprets the symbolic expression as an intentional paraphrase or transmogrification of a known thing is *allegoric*.[201]

Lewis stories hid explicit Christian theology within stories explicitly designed to express those values. Thus he was creating an allegory: "an intentional paraphrase or transmogrification of a known thing." In contrast, *The Lord of the Rings* was a true symbolic creation; the values Tolkien expressed emerged ineluctably from the necessary actions of his characters within the world he created. Though a deeply religious man, he felt strongly that there should be no overt expression of his religious beliefs in *The Lord of the Rings*. If these values were indeed eternal, they could best be seen simply through their realization in the lives of his characters, characters that he considered to be as real as any person we read about in history. Since each was forced in his own way to deal with the great darkness presented in the book, each person's story was necessarily a possible individual human solution to a more than human situation, a situation guaranteed to push each to his limits.

Tolkien had been deeply affected by the great mythological tales of many cultures: as a child, by the Fairy Books of Andrew Lang; as a school boy, the Old English poem, *Beowulf*; the Middle English poem, *Sir Gawain and the Green Knight*; the Finnish collection of poems, *Kalevala* (Land of Heros); as an undergraduate at Oxford, the Old Norse prose of *The Younger Eddas* and the collection of poetry known as *The Elder Eddas*. Those great stories sunk deep into Tolkien, there to be transformed, then emerge like dreams, to form the core of *The Lord of the Rings*. As Ursula le Guin tells us: "The great fantasies, myths and tales are indeed like dreams: they speak *from* the unconscious *to* the unconscious, in the *language* of the unconscious − symbol and archetype. Though they use words, they work the way music does: they short-circuit verbal reasoning, and go straight to the thoughts that lie too deep to utter."[202]

The words of these mythological stories themselves reflect the process of transformation within their very structure. Each of the words we use so casually in our everyday speech contains a rich history within itself. Words appear seemingly from nowhere, mutate over time, disappear suddenly, then reappear in some new guise or setting. Because we think largely in words, the words available to us structure the way we think and act. Tolkien understood this at some visceral level long before he could articulate it in his writing. His biographer, Humphrey Carpenter, points out that Tolkien's fascination with the roots of language first emerged when he was a schoolboy.

It was one thing to know Latin, Greek, French and German: it was another to understand *why* they were what they were. Tolkien had started to look for the bones, the elements that were common to them all: he had begun, in fact, to study philology, the science of words. And he was encouraged to do this even more when he made his acquaintance with Anglo-Saxon.[203]

In his writing, Tolkien was thus inspired not only by the stories these great myths told, but equally by their linguistic underpinnings, which determined *how they were told*. And, perhaps most important of all, because of his religious faith, he trusted enough to look deeply within and let his own creativity emerge. In doing so, Tolkien tapped archetypal roots that give *The Lord of the Rings* a resonance lacking in more contrived tales. He didn't feel that he was inventing lands, characters, and events: rather he was *discovering* them. Tolkien's goal was to create something that didn't exist: a full mythology for his beloved England that had all the majesty in found in these earlier archetypal tales. As he said of this earlier goal, recollecting it in his later days:

> Do not laugh! But once upon a time (my crest has long since fallen) I had a mind to make a body of more or less connected legend, ranging from the large and cosmogonic to the level of romantic fairy-story – the larger founded on the lesser in contact with the earth, the lesser drawing splendour from the vast backcloths – which I could dedicate simply: to England; to my country. . . I would draw some of the great tales in fullness, and leave many only placed in the scheme, and sketched. The cycles should be linked to a majestic whole, and yet leave scope for other minds and hands, wielding paint and music and drama. Absurd.[204]

The Lord of the Rings was thus only a part of his great goal, but what a part!

Endnotes

1.P. L. Travers, *What the Bee Knows: Reflections on Myth, Symbol and Story* (London: Penguin/Arkana, 1989), p. 297.

2.C. G. Jung, *Psychology and Alchemy, CW 12*, par. 32.

3.Marie-Louise von Franz, "Self-Realization in Individual Therapy," in *Psychotherapy* (Boston & London: Shambhala, 1993), p. 14.

4.Philip Pullman, Acceptance speech for 1995 Carnegie Medal for excellence in children's literature. Found on world wide web, at http://www.randomhouse.com/features/pullman/philippullman/spee ch.html.

5.Konrad Lorenz, *King Solomon's Ring* (New York: Time Incorporated, 1952), p.47.

6.Konrad Lorenz, *King Solomon's Ring*, p.48.

7.Quotation in Wechsler, Lawrence, *Mr. Wilson's Cabinet of Wonders*, p. 89.

8.Quotation in Wechsler, Lawrence, *Mr. Wilson's Cabinet of Wonders*, p. 89-90.

9.Quotation by John Horton Conway in Shulman, Polly, "Infinity Plus one, and Other Surreal Numbers," Discover Magazine, December 1995, p. 98.

10.III,510. Note that in the endnotes, I, II, and III refer respectively to: I - *The Fellowship of the Ring* (1954); II- *The Two Towers* (1954); and III - *The Return of the King* (1955). All volumes by J. R. R. Tolkien, published in Boston by Houghton Mifflin.

11.I,19.

12.I,15.

13.And Pippin would only have been11 years old!

14.I,121.

15.I,327.

16.I,344.

17.I,381.

18.II:16.

19.II,52.

20.II,66.

21.III,264.
22.William Cowper, *Poems* (London: J. Johnson, 1782-85).
23.II,66.
24.II,68.
25.(II,74).
26.II:196.
27.II:197.
28.II,204.
29.III,26
30.III,48.
31.III,145.
32.I,282.
33.I,309.
34.I 312.
35.I,321.
36.I,321.
37.I,336.
38.I,346.
39.I,346.
40.I,353-4.
41.I,372.
42.I,372.
43.I,380.
44.I,390.
45.I,411.

46.I,410.
47.I,411.
48.II,22.
49.Joseph Campbell, *The Hero With a Thousand Faces*, 2nd ed. (Princeton: Princeton University Press, Bollingen Series XVII, 1968) p.229.
50.II,35.

51.II,95.

52.II,129.

53.III,57.

54.III,58.

55.III,150.

56.III,257.

57.III,367.

58.I,46.

59.I,47.

60.I,50.

61.I,55.

62.I,65.

63.above history from Jorge Luis Borges, "Pascal's Sphere", in *Other Inquisitions: 1937-1952* (Austin: University of Texas Press, 1965), pp. 6-9.

64.I,74.

65.I,75.

66.I,286.

67.I,287.

68.I,297.

69.I,329.

70.I,362.

71.I,363.

72.II,99.

73.II,100.

74.II,106.

75.II,104.

76.II,116.

77.II,118.

78.II,119.

79.II,121.

80.II,122.

81.II,123.

82.II,184.

83.II,185.

84.II, 185-6.

85.II,187.

86.II,187.

87.III,85.

88.III,89.

89.III,167.

90.III,299.

91.I,177.

92.I,192.

93.Originally "hit is not al gold, that glareth" in Chaucer's *The House of Fame*; "all that glisters is not gold" in Shakespeare's *The Merchant of Venice*; "All, as they say, that glitters is not gold" in Dryden's *The Hind and the Panther* (first to use "glitters").

94.I,194.

95.I,194.

96.I,194.

97.I,207.

98.I,209.

99.I,245.

100.I,272.

101.I,273.

102.I,364.

103.I,429.

104.II,36.

105.II,145.

106.III,46.

107.III,56.

108.III,61.

109.III,136.

110.III,142.

111.III,249.

112.III,250.

113.III,348.

114.I,70.

115.I,68.

116.*The Hobbit*, 79.

117.*The Hobbit*, 82.

118.*The Hobbit*, 87.

119.II,219.

120.Bram Stoker, *Dracula* (1987), Ch. 3.

121.II,221.

122.I,74.

123.II,221.

124.II,224.

125.II,225.

126.II,228.

127.II,232.

128.II:235.

129.II:236.

130.II:238.

131.II:240.

132.II:249.

133.II:323.

134.III:224.

135.Humphrey Carpenter, *Tolkien: A Biography* (Boston: Houghton Mifflin Co, 1977), p. 81.

136.I,98, all quotes.

137.I,103, both quotes.

138.I,104.

139.I,299.

140.I,394.

141.I,397.

142.I,442.

143.II,209.

144.II,265.

145.II,269.

146.II,271.

147.II,271.

148.II,272.

149.II,288.

150.II,288.

151.II,289.

152.II,290.

153.II,319-20.

154.I,104.

155.II,349.

156.II,289.

157.Robin Robertson, *Your Shadow* (Virginia Beach: A.R.E. Press, 1997), p. 114.

158.Robin Robertson, *Your Shadow*, p. 115.

159.I, 54.

160.I,78.

161.I,100.

162.I,139.

163.Active Imagination is a method created by Jung to complement dream work. In its simplest form, one takes anything symbolic, such as a scene in a dream, or even a single image in a dream, and then lets it expand within oneself. This can be visual, simply letting a scene unfold, or oral, engaging in conversation with the image. There are many other possibilities. But the key is the word "active". One has to first let imagination have its way, but then second, one has to engage actively with what the imagination produces. This differs sharply from, for example, channeling, where one simply allows the unconscious to flow through oneself, with no intervention.

164.I,145.

165.I,149.

166.I,149.

167.I,150.

168.I,151.

169.I,169.

170.I,194.

171.I,298.

172.I,299.

173.I,390.

174.I.399.

175.I,400.

176.400.

177.III,226.

178.III,228.

179.III,303.

180.III,303.

181.III,303.

182.Tom Shippey, *J. R. R. Tolkien: Author of the Century* (Boston, New York: Houghton Mifflin, 2001), p. xvii.

183.Patrick Curry, *Defending Middle-Earth* (New York: HarperCollins, 1997), p. 12 for information on sales and translations, as of 1997.

184.Humphrey Carpenter, *Tolkien: A Biography*, p. 232.

185.George Sayer, "Recollections of J. R. R. Tolkien," in Joseph Pearce, ed., *Tolkien: A Celebration* (San Francisco: Ignatius Press, 1999), p. 15.

186.Ursula K. Le Guin, *The Language of the Night*, rev. ed., (New York: HarperCollins, 1989).

187.both quotes from Ursula K. Le Guin, *The Language of the Night*, p. 34.

188. J. R. R. Tolkien, "On Fairy Stories," in *Tree and Leaf*, included in *The Tolkien Reader*, (New York: Ballantine Books, 1966), pp. 60-1.

189.J. R. R. Tolkien, "On Fairy Stories," p. 63.

190.J. R. R. Tolkien, "On Fairy Stories," p. 54.

191.J. R. R. Tolkien, "On Fairy Stories," p. 55.

192.Humphrey Carpenter, *Tolkien: A Biography*, p. 101.

193.Humphrey Carpenter, *Tolkien: A Biography*, p. 201.

194.Humphrey Carpenter, *Tolkien: A Biography*, p. 148.

195.See Humphrey Carpenter, *Tolkien: A Biography*, pp. 143-8.

196.Humphrey Carpenter, *Tolkien: A Biography*, p. 131.

197.Humphrey Carpenter, *Tolkien: A Biography*, p. 151.

198.George Sayer, "Recollections of J. R. R. Tolkien," in Joseph Pearce, ed., *Tolkien: A Celebration* (San Francisco: Ignatius Press, 1999), p. 14.

199.J. R. R. Tolkien, *The Lord of the Rings*, vol. I, pp. 11-2.

200.C. G. Jung, *Psychological Types, CW6* (Princeton: Princeton University Press, Bollingen Series XX), par. 819.

201.C. G. Jung, *Psychological Types, CW6* (Princeton: Princeton University Press, Bollingen Series XX), pars. 814-5.

202.Ursula le Guin, *The Language of the Night*, p. 57.

203.Humphrey Carpenter, *Tolkien: A Biography*, p. 34.

204.Humphrey Carpenter, *Tolkien: A Biography*, pp. 89-90.

Printed in Poland
by Amazon Fulfillment
Poland Sp. z o.o., Wrocław

56623310R00107